KS2
Success

LEARN AND PRACTISE

Maths and English

Paul Broadbent and Alison Head

Contents

MATHS

2

Understanding shape

Measuring

Handling data

Glossary

Contents

ENGLISH

Speaking and listening

Reading

Writing

Glossary

Maths and English Answers

Word problems

Answering problems

If you have a word problem to solve, it may help to follow these stages.

Peter uses 500g of flour each day to make bread. A 1.5kg bag of flour costs him 86p. How much will he spend on flour to make bread for 12 days?

1   Read the problem.

Try to picture the problem and imagine going through it in real life.

3   Answer the calculations.

$500 \times 12 = 6000g = 6kg$
$6 \div 1.5 = 4$ bags
$86 \times 4 = 344$

2   Sort out the calculations.

$500g \times 12$ is the amount of flour he uses. Divide this by 1.5kg to work out the number of bags. Multiply 86p by the number of bags needed.

4   Answer the problem.

Look back at the question – what is it asking?
The cost of flour for bread for 12 days is £3.44.

Multi-step problems

Word problems can have different numbers of calculations to answer before you reach the final answer.

Two-step problems
A computer costs £985. It has a 10% discount in a sale. What is the new sale price?

Step 1   10% of £985 is £98.50.

Step 2
```
   985.00
 −  98.50
   886.50
```
The computer costs £886.50.

Three-step problems
Gemma bought a book of 45 stamps. She used $\frac{1}{5}$ of them on Monday and used 17 more on Tuesday. How many stamps does she have left?

Step 1	Step 2	Step 3
$\frac{1}{5}$ of $45 = 9$	$45 - 9 = 36$	$36 - 17 = 19$

Gemma has 19 stamps left.

Answering problems

1   Gemma saved £100 to spend on some clothes. She spent $\frac{2}{5}$ of her
    money in one shop. How much money did she have left?   £ [   ]

2   A flight had a baggage allowance of 32kg. A passenger had two
    cases and when one was placed on the scales it weighed 19.65kg.
    What is the maximum weight allowed for his other case?   [   ] kg

3   In a survey of 140 children, 15% of the children asked said that they
    had watched the news on television the previous evening.
    How many children in total had watched the news?   [   ]

4   These boxes are stored on a tray. Calculate the largest number
    of boxes that will fit on the tray, with no overlapping or stacked boxes.

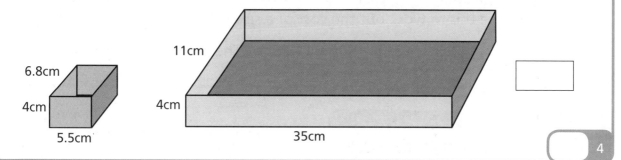

6.8cm
4cm
5.5cm

11cm
4cm
35cm

[   ]

4

Multi-step problems

1   278 people went to a school concert. They each paid a 75p
    entrance fee and 50% of them bought programmes for 40p.
    How much money was paid altogether?   £ [   ]

2   Circle the offer that sells bread rolls at the lowest individual price for a roll:

    Bag of 12 rolls: £2.24.   Bag of 6 rolls: £1.35.

    Offer: Buy 1 bag, get 1 bag half price.   Offer: Buy 2 bags, get 3rd bag free.

3   A pack of six golf balls, including the packaging, weighs a total
    of 298g. The packaging weighs 40g. What is the total weight of
    the pack if two of the balls are taken out?   [   ] g

4   Sam is having a party and needs enough chocolate bars for
    39 people. He buys packs of choc bars that cost £2.39 for 5 bars.
    How much will it cost to buy enough packs so
    that each person has a choc bar?   £ [   ]

4

TOTAL MARKS [   ] **8**

Problem-solving

USING AND APPLYING MATHEMATICS   LEARN

Reasoning

If you need to think carefully about a way to solve a problem, you are likely to be using reasoning skills to make sense of it. Some maths questions look simple, but involve a lot of thought. It may help to explain the problem to someone else, describing the way you could try to solve it.

> A drink and a sandwich together cost £2.55.
>
> Two drinks and a sandwich together cost £3.45.

What is the cost of a sandwich?

To answer this, work out the cost of a drink (the difference between the two prices), then use this to work out the cost of a sandwich.

> £3.45 − £2.55 = 90p   £2.55 − 90p = £1.65   The sandwich costs £1.65.

Finding all possibilities

These types of problems often have lots of choices of answers and the skill is finding the correct one. Work systematically, making lists of all possible answers to find the right one.

A group of 12 people book a trip to an aquarium. It costs £8, but some of the group pay only £5, as they are over 65 years old. The 12 people pay a total of £81. How many over-65s are in the group?

Draw a table to help you answer this.

Number of people	£8 entrance	£5 entrance
1	£8	£5
2	£16	£10
3	£24	£15
4	£32	£20
5	£40	**£25**
6	£48	£30
7	**£56**	£35

7 × £8 and 5 × £5 totals £81, so there are 5 over-65s in the group.

Look for a total of 12 people with a combined cost of £81.

Key words   difference

Reasoning

A and B each stand for a different number. A = 12.
What is the value of B for each of these?

1 A + A = A + B + B

2 A^2 + A = B + B

3 A (A + A) = B + A

4 A drink and a hot-dog together cost £1.25. Two drinks and
a hot-dog together cost £1.80. How much does a hot-dog cost? [ ]p

5 If you add a 3-digit number to a 3-digit number you cannot get a 5-digit
number. Is this true or false? Explain how you know.

_____

*Reasoning is all about thinking things through. Read
the questions a few times so that you can sort out a
strategy to answer the problem.*

5

Finding all possibilities

1 Circle the two consecutive numbers that give a product of 2256.

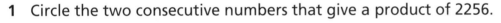

27   28   29   37   38   39   47   48   49

2 X and Y are two different whole numbers.
X + Y = 2000   X is 450 greater than Y.

X = [ ]   Y = [ ]

3 A necklace has white beads weighing 11 grams each and black beads
weighing 15 grams each. There are 12 beads altogether and the total
weight of the beads is 160g. How many black beads are there? [ ]

4 An isosceles triangle has a perimeter of 23cm. One of its
sides is 8.4cm. What are possible lengths of the
other two sides?
[ ] cm and [ ] cm

5 Which three prime numbers multiply to make 231? [ ] × [ ] × [ ] = 231

5

TOTAL MARKS [ ] 10

Rules and patterns

Number sequences

A sequence is a list of numbers which usually have a pattern. You can often find the pattern or rule in a sequence by looking at the difference between the numbers.

What is the next number in the sequence?   42   27   12   −3   −18   ____

Each number is 15 less than the previous one, so the next number is − 33. The rule is 'subtract 15'.

Formulae and equations

A formula (plural is formulae) uses letters or words to give a rule.

What is the rule for this sequence of numbers?

A	1	2	3	4	5	n
B	4	7	10	13	16	?

Look at the relationship between the pairs of numbers. The numbers in row A are multiplied by 3 and then 1 is added to make each of the numbers in row B. So for n, the formula is $3n + 1$. You can use this to find any number in the pattern. What is the 15th number in the sequence? $3 \times 15 + 1 = 46$.

Equations have symbols or letters instead of numbers in a calculation.

$\blacksquare + 2 = 15$ $4\blacktriangle − 5 = 19$ $3y + 9 = 24$

You need to work out what the symbol or letter stands for, so use the numbers given to help you.

Top Tip *Equations need to stay balanced. If you add or take away a number from one side, do the same to the other side, so the equation stays the same. It's a good way of working out the letter.*

Try working it out step-by-step. $3y + 9 = 24$

1   You want y on one side of the equation and the numbers on the other. Subtract 9 from both sides. If it were −9, you would add 9 to both sides.
$3y = 24 − 9$ $3y = 15$

2   Say the equation as a sentence: 3 times something makes 15. So $y = 5$.

3   Test it with the original equation: $(3 \times 5) + 9 = 24$.

Key words   sequence   formula   equation

Number sequences

Write the pattern or rule for each sequence for one mark. Then underline yes or no for each question for a second mark.

1   −6   −1   4   9   14   the rule is _____

Will 99 be in this sequence?   yes / no

2   −8   −5   −2   1   4   the rule is _____

Will 30 be in this sequence?   yes / no

3   20   14   8   2   − 4   the rule is _____

Will −20 be in this sequence?   yes / no

4   11   7   3   −1   −5   the rule is _____

Will −21 be in this sequence?   yes / no

5   −52   −22   8   38   68   the rule is _____

Will 180 be in this sequence?   yes / no

10

Formulae and equations

Work out the value of each letter.

1 $3h + 2 = 26$ ☐   **2** $4y − 5 = 11$ ☐   **3** $2r + 1 = 15$ ☐

4 Callum made a shape pattern with counters. The table shows the number of counters he used for each shape.

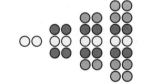

Shape number	1	2	3	4	n
Counters	2	6	10	14	?

Tick the correct formula for this shape pattern.

$3n − 1$ ☐ $2n + 2$ ☐ $4n − 2$ ☐ $5n − 3$ ☐ $3n + 1$ ☐

5 Callum uses 58 counters to make a shape in this pattern.

What is its shape number? ☐

Top Tip — **3y** *means* **y** *multiplied by 3. The* **x** *sign for multiplication is not used in equations, because it might look like a letter.*

5

TOTAL MARKS 15

Comparing and ordering

Ordering decimals

Putting decimals in order is just like putting whole numbers in order – you need to look carefully at the value of each digit.

These are the times for the women's 50m freestyle swimming final at an Olympics. What order did they finish the race in?

Swimmer	Time (seconds)
Michelle Engelsman, Australia	25.06
Kara Lynn Joyce, United States	25.00
Inge de Bruijn, Netherlands	24.58
Libby Lenton, Australia	24.91
Therese Alshammar, Sweden	24.93
Malia Metella, France	24.89

Write them out one under the other.

25.06
25.00
24.58
24.91
24.93
24.89

Compare the digits from left to right, re-ordering the numbers so that the smallest number is first.

24.58
24.89
24.91
24.93
25.00
25.06

 Top Tip *Remember to line up the decimal points.*

Negative numbers

Positive numbers are above zero and negative numbers are below zero.

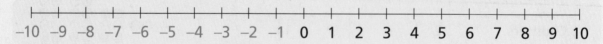

$$-10 \quad -9 \quad -8 \quad -7 \quad -6 \quad -5 \quad -4 \quad -3 \quad -2 \quad -1 \quad 0 \quad 1 \quad 2 \quad 3 \quad 4 \quad 5 \quad 6 \quad 7 \quad 8 \quad 9 \quad 10$$

We can compare numbers by looking at their positions on the number line.

Look at the differences between these pairs of temperatures.

inside	outside	difference
6°C	−4°C	10°C
12°C	−7°C	19°C
−1°C	−9°C	8°C

 Key words   digit   negative number

Ordering decimals

Use the four digits and the decimal point to answer these questions.
There must be one digit in front of the decimal point.

| 4 | 8 | 9 | 1 | • |

1 What is the largest decimal number you can make?   ___ • ___ ___ ___

2 What is the smallest decimal number you can make?   ___ • ___ ___ ___

3 Make a decimal number as near as possible to 9.   ___ • ___ ___ ___

4 Make a decimal number between 1.5 and 1.9.   ___ • ___ ___ ___

5 Write all the decimal numbers you have made in order, from smallest to largest.

smallest   **largest**

5

Negative numbers

What is the difference in temperature between these pairs of thermometers?

1   _____ °

2   _____ °

3   _____ °

4 Circle the two numbers with a difference of 18.

   −9   −7   8   7   13   −11

5 Write these temperatures in order, starting with the lowest.

   8.5°C   6°C   −8°C   −4°C   −11°C   1.5°C

smallest   **largest**

5

TOTAL MARKS   10

Fractions

Equivalent fractions

Equivalent fractions have different numerators and denominators, but are worth the same value.

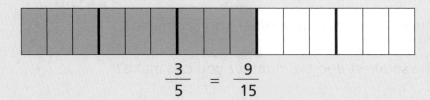

$$\frac{3}{5} = \frac{9}{15}$$

A fraction can be changed into its equivalent by multiplying the numerator and denominator by the same amount.

$3 \times 3 = 9$ $5 \times 3 = 15$

You can reduce a fraction to an equivalent fraction by dividing the top and bottom by the highest common factor – the biggest number that will divide into both.

$$\frac{18}{24} = \frac{3}{4}$$ $18 \div 6 = 3$ $24 \div 6 = 4$

$\frac{3}{4}$ is a fraction in its lowest terms, or simplest form.

Comparing fractions

If fractions have the same denominator, they are easy to compare.

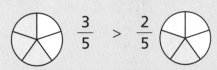

$$\frac{3}{5} > \frac{2}{5}$$

To compare fractions with different denominators, change them to equivalent fractions with a common denominator – the same denominator.

Which is the larger fraction, $\frac{2}{3}$ or $\frac{3}{4}$?

Find the equivalent fractions to $\frac{2}{3}$ and $\frac{3}{4}$ that have a common denominator.

$\frac{2}{3} = \frac{4}{6} = \frac{6}{9} = \frac{8}{12}$ $\frac{3}{4} = \frac{6}{8} = \frac{9}{12}$

$\frac{9}{12}$ is larger than $\frac{8}{12}$, so $\frac{3}{4}$ is larger than $\frac{2}{3}$.

Top Tip You can also compare fractions by changing them to decimals.

 Key words   numerator   denominator   highest common factor

common denominator

Equivalent fractions

Write the fraction in its simplest form for the shaded part of each shape.

1 [ ]

2 [ ]

3 [ ]

4 [ ]

5 [ ]

[5]

Comparing fractions

Look at these number cards.

    3   2   8   7   5

1 Use two of the number cards to complete this: $\dfrac{\square}{\square} > \dfrac{1}{2}$

2 Use four of the number cards to complete this: 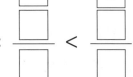 $\dfrac{\square}{\square} < \dfrac{\square}{\square}$

3 Which is larger, $\frac{2}{3}$ or $\frac{4}{5}$? Explain how you know.

_____

4 Write a fraction that lies between $\frac{1}{4}$ and $\frac{3}{8}$. $\dfrac{\square}{\square}$

5 Write a fraction that could complete this: 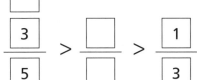 $\dfrac{3}{5} > \dfrac{\square}{\square} > \dfrac{1}{3}$

[5]

TOTAL MARKS [ ] 10

Fractions, decimals, percentages

Percentages and fractions

Percentages are simply fractions out of 100 – that is what per cent means: out of 100.

% is the percentage sign.

In a tile pattern of 100 tiles, 25 are red.
25% of the tiles are red, which is $\frac{1}{4}$ of the tiles.

Another tile pattern of 20 tiles has 5 red tiles. This also means 25% of the tiles are red.

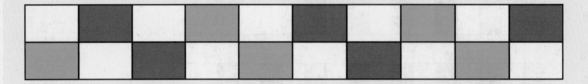

To change fractions to percentages, make them out of 100. This means you need to find an **equivalent fraction** with the denominator 100.

$\frac{3}{5}$ is equivalent to $\frac{60}{100}$, so $\frac{3}{5} = 60\%$.

To change per cent to fraction, write the percentage as a fraction out of 100 and then reduce to its lowest terms.

40% is $\frac{40}{100}$, which is the same as $\frac{2}{5}$.

5% is $\frac{5}{100}$, which is the same as $\frac{1}{20}$.

 Top Tip *If you find it easier, write the fraction as a decimal and then multiply by 100.*
$\frac{3}{4}$ is 0.75, which is the same as 75%.

Equivalent values

It is a good idea to memorise these. Cover up different boxes and work out the covered amounts.

Decimals	0.1	0.2	0.3	0.4	0.5	0.6	0.7	0.8	0.9	0.25	0.75
Fractions	$\frac{1}{10}$	$\frac{1}{5}$	$\frac{3}{10}$	$\frac{2}{5}$	$\frac{1}{2}$	$\frac{3}{5}$	$\frac{7}{10}$	$\frac{4}{5}$	$\frac{9}{10}$	$\frac{1}{4}$	$\frac{3}{4}$
Percent	10%	20%	30%	40%	50%	60%	70%	80%	90%	25%	75%

 Key words   percentage   equivalent fraction

Percentages and fractions

These are Josh's maths test scores as marks out of a total. Convert each of the scores to percentages.

1 7 out of 10 = ☐ %

2 16 out of 20 = ☐ %

3 38 out of 50 = ☐ %

4 20 out of 25 = ☐ %

☐ 4

Equivalent values

Write the missing numbers to complete these.

1 $\dfrac{1}{\boxed{}} = 0.\boxed{} = 50\%$

2 $\dfrac{\boxed{}}{4} = 0.25 = \boxed{}\%$

3 $\dfrac{1}{20} = 0.\boxed{} = \boxed{}\%$

4 $\dfrac{2}{\boxed{}} = 0.4 = \boxed{}\%$

5 $\dfrac{17}{50} = 0.\boxed{} = \boxed{}\%$

6 $\dfrac{7}{\boxed{}} = 0.7 = \boxed{}\%$

7 $\dfrac{\boxed{}}{100} = 0.09 = \boxed{}\%$

8 $\dfrac{11}{\boxed{}} = 0.44 = \boxed{}\%$

Write <, > or = to make each statement true.

9 25% ☐ 0.25

10 0.2 ☐ 20%

11 0.75 ☐ 57%

12 4% ☐ 0.4

13 8% ☐ 0.8

14 0.1 ☐ 10%

15 7% ☐ 0.07

16 $\dfrac{2}{5}$ ☐ 0.4

 Top Tip *If you are asked to convert a percentage to a decimal, remember that it will always be less than 1.*

☐ 16

Ratio

Ratio

Ratio is used to compare one amount with another.

What is the ratio of green to orange tiles?

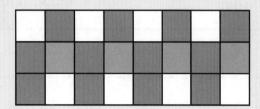

There are 4 green tiles and 12 orange tiles. For every 1 green tile, there are 3 orange tiles. The ratio of green to orange is 1 to 3, or 1:3.

This ratio stays the same for different amounts:

Green	1	2	3	4	5	6
Orange	3	6	9	12	15	18

How many green tiles are needed if 60 tiles are used in this pattern?

The proportion of tiles that are green is 1 in every 6, or $\frac{1}{6}$.

This means that in a set of 60 tiles, 10 would be green.

Ratios are a bit like fractions – they can both be simplified by finding the highest common factors. For example, in a class of 16 boys and 12 girls, the ratio of boys to girls is 16:12. This can be simplified by dividing by 4 to give a ratio of 4:3.

Top Tip

Direct proportion

Two quantities are in direct proportion when they increase or decrease in the same ratio. For example, if 3 pens cost 90p, what is the cost of 15 pens?

This is 5 times the number of pens, so it is five times the price. 90p × 5 = £4.50.

Scale drawings and maps are examples of ways we use direct proportion.

This car is drawn at a scale of 50:1. The drawing is 4.6cm long. How long is the actual car?

4.6cm x 50 = 230cm = 2.3m

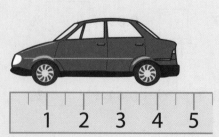

Key words   ratio   proportion

Ratio

1 Ali shares out 24 sweets. He gives Sophie 1 sweet for every 3 he takes. How many sweets does Sophie get?

2 Hannah puts some tulips, daffodils and carnations in a vase. For every one tulip, she uses three daffodils and four carnations. She uses 40 flowers altogether. How many daffodils does she use?

3 Daniel mixes 1 litre of white paint with every 4 litres of green paint. He needs 20 litres of paint altogether. How many litres of green paint will he need?

4 Robert pours 1 carton of orange juice and 1 carton of cranberry juice into a jug. He wants only half as much orange juice as cranberry juice in the mixture. What should he pour into his jug now? _____

5 An 80g snack bar has 80% oats and 20% fruit. What is the ratio of oats to fruit in a bar, in its simplest form? _____

5

Direct proportion

In this recipe the amount of each ingredient is given as a proportion of the total weight.

1 Write the weight of each ingredient into the recipe.

2 Using this recipe, how many grams of butter would be needed for a 900g cake? _____

3 Here is a rectangle with six identical shaded squares in it. The width is 4.5cm. What is the length of the rectangle?

_____

4 Six toy cars cost a total of £4.50. What is the cost of ten cars? _____

5 A 1.2 litre jug of lemon squash is mixed in the proportion of $\frac{1}{10}$ fruit juice to $\frac{9}{10}$ water. How much juice is in the jug when it is half full? _____

600g Carrot and Walnut Cake

$\frac{1}{4}$ butter → 150 g

$\frac{1}{3}$ flour → ☐ g

$\frac{1}{6}$ grated carrots → ☐ g

$\frac{1}{10}$ sugar → ☐ g

$\frac{1}{12}$ beaten eggs → ☐ g

$\frac{1}{15}$ walnuts → ☐ g

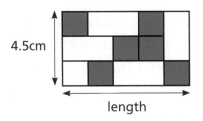

4.5cm

length

5

Multiples and factors

Factors

Factors are numbers that will divide exactly into other numbers. It is useful to put factors of numbers into pairs:

> Factors of 30 ➜ (1,30), (2,15), (3,10), (5,6) = 8 factors
>
> Factors of 45 ➜ (1,45), (315), (5,9) = 6 factors

If you look at the factors of 30 and 45, there are some factors that are the same for both numbers. The numbers 1, 3, 5 and 15 are common factors of 30 and 45.

15 is the largest number which is a common factor of 30 and 45, which means that the Highest Common Factor (written as HCF) of 30 and 45 is 15.

 Highest common factors are used to simplify equivalent fractions. For example, $\frac{32}{56}$ can be simplified to $\frac{4}{7}$ by dividing by the HCF of 32 and 56, which is 8.

Multiples

A multiple is a number made by multiplying together two other numbers.

Look at these multiples of 6 and 8.

> Multiples of 6 ➜ 6, 12, 18, **24**, 30, 36...
>
> Multiples of 8 ➜ 8, 16, **24**, 32, 40, 48...

The Lowest Common Multiple (LCM) of 6 and 8 is 24.

Prime factors

A prime number only has two factors: 1 and itself. For example, 23 is a prime number, as it can only be divided by 1 and 23. The number 1 is **not** a prime number, as it only has one factor.

The prime factors of a number are all those factors of the number which are prime numbers.

All the factors of 28 are 1, 2, 4, 7, 14 and 28. The prime factors of 28 are 2 and 7.

 Key words

| factor | highest common factor | multiple |
| lowest common multiple | prime number | prime factor |

Factors

List the common factors for each of these. Underline the HCF for each set.

1 Common factors of 12 and 42. _____

2 Common factors of 15 and 45. _____

3 Common factors of 14 and 42. _____

4 Common factors of 36, 42 and 48. _____

5 Common factors of 12, 24 and 30. _____

[5]

Multiples

Write the numbers **2**, **3**, **4**, **5**, **6** or **9** to complete these statements.

1 92 is a multiple of ☐ and ☐.

2 117 is a multiple of ☐ and ☐.

3 280 is a multiple of ☐, ☐ and ☐.

4 84 is a multiple of ☐, ☐, ☐ and ☐.

5 432 is a multiple of ☐, ☐, ☐, ☐ and ☐.

6 9180 is a multiple of ☐, ☐, ☐, ☐, ☐ and ☐.

7 What is the lowest common multiple of 9 and 4? ☐

Top Tip — *To work out multiples of different numbers, use rules of divisibility. e.g. 92 cannot be divided by 3, because the digits of 92 do not total 3, 6 or 9. So 92 is not a multiple of 3.*

[7]

Prime factors

Choose any of these factors to complete the multiplications.

3   4   5   7   11   13

1 ☐ × ☐ × ☐ = 84   3 ☐ × ☐ × ☐ = 715

2 ☐ × ☐ × ☐ = 132

[3]

TOTAL MARKS [15]

Estimating answers

Rounding decimals

Rounding decimals makes them easier to work with. For example, this bag weighs 6.372 kilograms.

This is very exact and you probably only need to know that it is about 6kg, or if you want to be a little more accurate, it weighs about 6.4kg.

Decimals are usually rounded to the nearest whole number or nearest tenth.

Rounding to the nearest whole number:	Rounding to the nearest tenth:
• Look at the tenths digit.	• Look at the hundredths digit.
• If it is 5 or more, round up to the next whole number.	• If it is 5 or more, round up to the next tenth.
• If it is less than 5, the units digit stays the same.	• If it is less than 5, the tenths digit stays the same.
16.5 rounds up to 17.	13.77 rounds up to 13.8.
7.48 rounds down to 7.	4.639 rounds down to 4.6.

Top Tip This is called rounding to a number of decimal places. If you have a question that asks you to round to 1 decimal place, it means round the number to the nearest tenth. If you are asked to round to 2 decimal places, it means round to the nearest hundredth.

Approximate answers

When you add, subtract, multiply or divide large numbers or decimals, it is always a good idea to estimate an approximate answer first. After you have worked out the answer, look back at the estimate to check that your answer makes sense.

Three plants cost £15.83, £7.36 and £24.19. What change will there be from £50?

Approximate total ➜ £16 + £7 + £24 = £47. So the change will be approximately £3.

```
   15.83
    7.36
+ 24.19
─────────
  £47.38      £50 − £47.38 = £2.62
```

 Key words   estimate   approximate

Rounding decimals

1 Join each of the decimals to the nearest tenth on the number line.

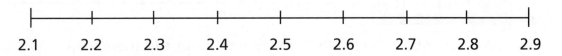

2.1   2.2   2.3   2.4   2.5   2.6   2.7   2.8   2.9

2.38   2.07   2.41   2.75   2.66   2.83

Round each of these to the nearest whole number:

2 14.063 → ☐

3 9.602 → ☐

4 23.009 → ☐

5 18.518 → ☐

6 27.905 → ☐

 6

Approximate answers

1 Can you circle the two numbers which, when multiplied together, have the answer closest to 60?

7.3   9.3   10.4   6.5

2 Circle the best estimate of $84.34 \div 11.86$.

5   6   7   8   9   10   11

3 What is the approximate total of 3 jugs, each holding 5.485 litres?
Write your answer to the nearest tenth of a litre.   _____

4 Four items from a market stall cost £2.58, £1.94, 78p and £4.03.
What will be the approximate change from £10?
Write your answer to the nearest 10p.   _____

5 True or false? $3.018 + 3.81$ gives a greater total than $3.801 + 3.18$.   _____

6 Spot the odd one out. Which of these answers is not
approximately 55 to the nearest whole number?
Cross out the odd one and write the number it rounds to.

$13.68 + 41.41$ $97.38 - 42.19$ 11.78×5.19 $109.89 \div 2$ _____

 6

TOTAL MARKS   12

Addition and subtraction

Adding decimals

When you have numbers to add, look to see if you can add them mentally. If they are large decimals, use a written method if you are not able to use a calculator.

When you add decimals, remember to line up the decimal points.

> What is the total of 14.9, 7.24 and 0.85?
>
> An approximate answer is 15 + 7 + 1 = 23.

 Top Tip *Put zeros in to even up the number of decimal places.*

1   Write them in a column, lining up the decimal points. Start by adding from the right-hand column.

```
   14.90
    7.24
 +  0.85
 _____
       9
```

2   Keep going left until all the columns have been added.

```
   14.90
    7.24
 +  0.85
 _____
   22.99
     11
```

```
   14.90
    7.24
  +0.85
```

Subtracting decimals

Check to see if you can work it out mentally before trying a written method.

> 9.4 – 3.76   An approximate answer is 9 – 4 = 5.

1   Write them in a column, lining up the decimal points. Start from the right-hand column and take away the bottom **digit** from the top digit.

```
   9.³4¹0
 – 3. 7 6
 _____
        4
```

If needed, remember to exchange a hundredth from the tenths column, renaming the numbers.

2   Now do the same with the other columns. Write it nice and clearly, so you can see the exchange and renaming of numbers.

```
   ⁸9 .¹³4¹0
 –  3 . 7 6
 _____
    5 . 6 4
```

 Key words   digit

Adding decimals

Write an approximate answer and then work out the exact answer.

1   412.79 + 178.16

2   Total 1.717 and 4.355.

3   Add 29.08 to 38.44.

4   What is the sum of 235.88 and 129.26?

5   What is the total of 2.845, 3.991 and 4.605?

Use the numbers in the grid to answer these.

6   Find four pairs of numbers that total 5.

   _____

7   Find four pairs of numbers that total 8.

   _____

2.792	2.614	3.281	4.212
4.183	1.175	3.817	1.943
3.825	2.208	5.179	2.386
1.719	3.788	6.057	2.821

7

Subtracting decimals

Look at the parcels and answer these.

 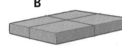    

A   B   C   D   E   F

A 3.245kg   B 11.88kg   C 2.915kg   D 4.203kg   E 12.79kg   F 16.24kg

1   What is the difference in weight between parcels F and B?   _____

2   How much more does parcel D weigh than parcel A?   _____

3   How much less does parcel E weigh than parcel F?   _____

4   Which parcel weighs 0.33kg less than parcel A?   _____

5   Which two parcels have a difference in weight of 0.91kg?   _____

5

TOTAL MARKS   12

Multiplication

Column method of multiplication

If the numbers are too large to multiply mentally, a column method or a grid method can be used.

This is the column method. Always estimate an approximate answer first.

What is 387 multiplied by 43? 387×43 is approximately $400 \times 40 = 16000$.

```
      387                → leading to →          387
   ×   43                                     ×   43
   ───────                                    ───────
    12000   (300 × 40)                         15480   (387 × 40)
     3200   (80 × 40)                           1161   (387 × 3)
      280   (7 × 40)                           ───────
      900   (300 × 3)                          16641
      240   (80 × 3)
       21   (7 × 3)
   ───────
    16641
```

Grid method

For this method, the numbers are partitioned into hundreds, tens and ones, and written around a grid. Multiply each pair of numbers to complete the grid and add up each row to find the total.

What is 387 multiplied by 43?

×	300	80	7		
40	12000	3200	280	→	15480
3	900	240	21	→	1161

Total: 16641

This method can be used to multiply 2, 3 or 4 digit numbers. Remember to estimate an answer first.

Key words   partition

Column method of multiplication

Use the column method of multiplying to answer these.

1 438 × 17 = _____

2 392 × 23 = _____

3 286 × 34 = _____

Write the missing digit for each part of the sum.

4 2 ___3 × 34 = 860 ___

5 ___15 × 29 = 1203 ___

6 517 × ___2 = 1654 ___

6

PRACTISE

Grid method

Use the grid method of multiplying to answer these.

1 294 × 18 = ☐

2 367 × 24 = ☐

3 293 × 35 = ☐

Choose your preferred method to answer these.

4 There are 125 computer discs in a box. How many computer discs are there in 38 boxes?

5 Daniel travels a total of 37.8km going to and from work each day. How far does he travel in five days?

6 A garden is 29 metres long and 9.8 metres wide. What is the area of the garden?

7 Sally saved £12.50 a week for 35 weeks. How much has she saved altogether?

8 Taking a shower uses approximately 35 litres of water. If you have a shower every day for a year, how much water would that use?

9 A small bottle of vinegar contains 455ml. An extra large bottle contains eight times as much. How many litres does the extra large bottle of vinegar hold?

9

TOTAL MARKS 15

Division

Written methods

Before you start on a written division, work out an approximate answer first.

What is 889 divided by 6?

889 ÷ 6 is approximately 900 ÷ 6, so it will be a little less than 150.

Remember, if a number cannot be divided exactly, it leaves a remainder.

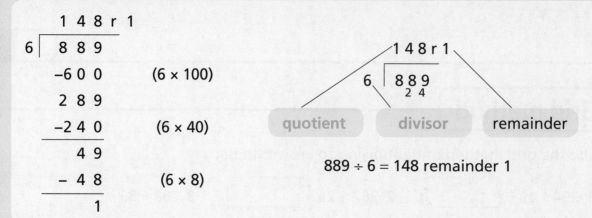

```
      1 4 8 r 1
  6 | 8 8 9
     -6 0 0        (6 × 100)
      2 8 9
     -2 4 0        (6 × 40)
        4 9
      -  4 8       (6 × 8)
           1
```

quotient   divisor   remainder

889 ÷ 6 = 148 remainder 1

Quotients as decimals

With some division questions, particularly with money or measures, the answer is not correct with a remainder. An exact number is needed with a decimal answer. Use the short method shown above, but put a decimal point and zeros after the decimal point, so that you can continue dividing the number.

£796 is divided amongst four people. How much do they each get?

```
       1 9 2 . 2 5
  4 | 7 6 9 . 0 0
       3     1 2
```

How many fours in 7 hundreds?   1 hundred, with 3 hundreds remaining.

How many fours in 36 tens?   9 tens.

How many fours in 9?   2, with 1 remaining.

How many fours in 10 tenths?   2 tenths, with 2 tenths remaining.

How many fours in 20 hundredths?   5 hundredths.

Key words   remainder   quotient   divisor

Written methods

Answer these problems.

1 A reel of electric cable is 500m in length. It is cut into 9m
   lengths. How many complete 9m lengths will there be?

2 A floor is 324cm long and floor tiles are 8cm in length.
   How many tiles will be needed to cover one whole
   length of the wall?

3 A schoolbook has 376 pages. There are six pages in each chapter.
   How many pages are left over for the contents and answers?

4 Seven beans are planted in a row. There are 162 beans in
   a packet. How many full rows can be planted from this
   packet of beans?

5 A farmer collects 249 eggs and puts them into egg boxes
   that hold 6 eggs. All the eggs must be in an egg box.
   How many egg boxes will he need?

*Top Tip: Look carefully at the question
to see if the remainder needs to
round up or down for the answer.*

5

Quotients as decimals

1 This piece of wood is divided into 4 equal lengths. How long is each length?

173cm

2 A group of 5 people win a prize of £2342 and share it equally
   between themselves. How much do they each get?

3 A water tank holds 182 litres. It is emptied and exactly fills 8
   large containers. What is the capacity of each container?

4 David saves the same amount each week. After 12 weeks he
   has saved £81. How much does he save each week?

5 A lorry holds 1293kg of grain. It is divided equally into
   5 containers. How much grain is in each container?

5

TOTAL MARKS 10

Fractions of quantities

Fractions and division

Finding fractions of quantities is very similar to dividing amounts.

Look at these examples. What is:

$\frac{1}{3}$ of 21? $\frac{1}{10}$ of 30?

These both have 1 as a **numerator**, so simply divide by the **denominator**.

$\frac{1}{3}$ of 21 is $21 \div 3 = 7$ $\frac{1}{10}$ of 30 is $30 \div 10 = 3$

Numerator greater than 1

$\frac{1}{8}$ of 40 = 5.

This is easy because we just divide by the denominator: $40 \div 8 = 5$.

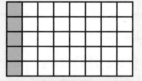

$\frac{5}{8}$ of 40 = 25

Now the numerator is 5, it means we count five of the groups.

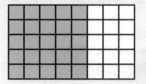

If the numerator is more than 1, divide by the denominator and then multiply by the numerator.

Look at these examples.

$\frac{2}{3}$ of 18 is $18 \div 3 = 6$, then $\times 2 = 12$

$\frac{3}{5}$ of 80 is $80 \div 5 = 16$, then $\times 3 = 48$

$\frac{7}{10}$ of 90 is $90 \div 10 = 9$, then $\times 7 = 63$

numerator?
denominator?

Top Tip *Try to work these out mentally, jotting down the division to keep a record for each part of the calculation.*

 Key words   numerator   denominator

Fractions and division

1 Mr Adams has a total of **96** farm animals. Write the number of each farm animal owned by Mr Adams.

$\frac{1}{2}$ are chickens   48

$\frac{1}{4}$ are goats   24

$\frac{1}{6}$ are cows   ☐

$\frac{1}{12}$ are ducks   ☐

Answer these.

2 What fraction of £1 is:	**3** What fraction of £2 is:	**4** What fraction of £10 is:
50p _____	20p _____	£2.50 _____
20p _____	£1 _____	£5 _____
10p _____	50p _____	£1 _____
25p _____	£1.50 _____	£7.50 _____
75p _____	40p _____	£2 _____

4

Numerator greater than 1

Write < or > between each pair of amounts.

1 $\frac{5}{8}$ of 32 ☐ $\frac{3}{4}$ of 32   **3** $\frac{3}{4}$ of 48 ☐ $\frac{5}{6}$ of 48

2 $\frac{2}{3}$ of 60 ☐ $\frac{3}{5}$ of 60   **4** $\frac{6}{7}$ of 28 ☐ $\frac{3}{4}$ of 28

Join the matching questions and answers.

5 190   **6** 342   **7** 268   **8** 291   **9** 301

$\frac{2}{3}$ of 402 $\frac{3}{4}$ of 456 $\frac{3}{5}$ of 485 $\frac{5}{8}$ of 304 $\frac{7}{10}$ of 430

9

TOTAL MARKS ☐ 13

Percentages of quantities

Percentages of a quantity

What is 20% of £320?

There are several methods you could use to solve this type of percentage question.

Method 1
Change to a fraction and work it out:

$20\% = \frac{20}{100} = \frac{1}{5}$

$\frac{1}{5}$ of £320 = £320 ÷ 5 = £64

Method 2
Use 10% to work it out – just divide the number by 10:

10% of £320 is £32. So, 20% of £32 is double that: £64.

Method 3
If you are allowed, use a calculator to work it out:

Key in:

20 ÷ 100 × 320 = ☐

Top Tip *To find 5%, remember that it is half of 10%.*

TV only £320

Percentage decreases and increases

Discounts and sales often have percentage decreases.

A car costing £5600 has a 10% discount. What is the sale price?

Step 1
Work out the percentage:

10% of £5600 is £560.

Step 2
Take away this amount from the price:

£5600 – £560 = £5040

So the sale price of the car is £5040.

For a percentage increase, there are still two steps, but you add the percentage to the price.

A bottle normally has 920ml of sauce, but this is increased by 5%. How much sauce is now in the bottle?

Step 1
Work out the percentage:

5% of 920ml is 46ml.

Step 2
Add this to the original amount:

920 + 46 is 966
So the new amount is 966ml.

 Key words | percentage

Percentages of a quantity

Write the percentages of each of these amounts.

1 £50

10% → £ ☐

30% → £ ☐

2 £80

10% → £ ☐

40% → £ ☐

3 £25

10% → £ ☐

30% → £ ☐

4 £200

10% → £ ☐

1% → £ ☐

5 £40

10% → £ ☐

5% → £ ☐

6 £2700

1% → £ ☐

2% → £ ☐

7 £6000

1% → £ ☐

12% → £ ☐

8 £180

5% → £ ☐

15% → £ ☐

☐ 8

Percentage decreases and increases

1 Last year there were 350 scouts at a scout parade. This year there were 20% fewer scouts. How many scouts were there in total this year?

2 A barrel of oil holds 300 litres when full. 25% of the oil is used up. How many litres of oil are still in the barrel?

3 960 chairs are put in a hall for a show on Tuesday night. 30% fewer chairs are needed the following night. How many chairs are needed in total on the Wednesday night?

4 A car is being sold for £3600. The car dealer decides to reduce the price by 5%. What is its new price?

Write the new amounts for each of these.

5

ORIGINALLY 450g

NOW 20% MORE!

6

OLD SIZE 520ml

NOW

25% MORE

7

LAST MONTH 240 pages.

THIS MONTH 15% MORE!

New box: ☐ g

New bottle: ☐ ml

New total of pages: ☐

☐ 7

TOTAL MARKS ☐ 15

Calculators

Using a calculator

Make sure you know how to use these keys on a calculator.

[+/-] changes a positive number to a negative number

[C] or [CE] clears the last entry – useful if you make a mistake halfway through a sum.

[%] percentage, e.g. to find 40% of £60, key in [6] [0] [×] [4] [0] [%] £24. Don't press [=].

[√] square root (inverse of a square number), e.g. to find the square root of 144, press [1] [4] [4] then the [√] key.

[AC] clears all entries and leaves [0].

Squares and square roots

Numbers multiplied by themselves make square numbers: $3 \times 3 = 9$. A short way of writing 3×3 is 3^2, which is 3 squared.

Square roots ($\sqrt{}$) are the opposite to square numbers. To find the square root of 25, find which number, when multiplied by itself, makes 25. So $\sqrt{25} = 5$. The square root key on calculators is useful for finding square roots that are not whole numbers. For example, we know the square root of 90 will be between 9 ($\sqrt{81}$) and 10 ($\sqrt{100}$). The calculator gives the actual number: 9.487.

Using brackets

When part of a problem is in brackets, you work out the bracket part first.

$15 - (8 + 4)$ $(15 - 8) + 4$

$15 - 12 = 3$ $7 + 4 = 11$

 Top Tip
Many calculators have different keys, so get used to the one you have and practise different calculations.

Calculators will ignore brackets unless you have a calculator with a bracket key, so make sure you key this part of the calculation first and write it down or put it into the calculator memory. Try the calculations above on your calculator.

 Key words square number square root

Using a calculator

Use a calculator to work out the missing numbers.

1 $445.48 \div \boxed{} = 8.6$ **3** $30528 \div \boxed{} = 384$

2 $34.7 \times \boxed{} = 631.54$

Here is a plan of a garden.

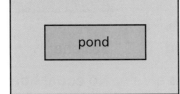

pond

17m 50cm

29m 20cm

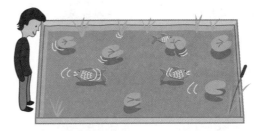

4 What is the area of the whole garden, including the pond? $\boxed{}$ m²

5 The pond takes up 20% of the garden.
What is the area of the pond? $\boxed{}$ m²

5

Squares and square roots

1 Each side of a square is 435mm.
What is the area of the square in square centimetres? $\boxed{}$

2 A square has an area of 729cm². What is the length of each side? $\boxed{}$ cm

3 Calculate the square root of each of these.

$\sqrt{324}$ $\boxed{}$ **4** $\sqrt{1369}$ $\boxed{}$ **5** $\sqrt{70.56}$ $\boxed{}$

5

Using brackets

Answer these.

1 $250 - (27.79 + 15.66) = \boxed{}$ **4** $35.9 - (18 \times 0.2) = \boxed{}$

2 $51.6 \times (3.44 + 6.9) = \boxed{}$ **5** $0.7 \times (38.6 - 19.8) = \boxed{}$

3 $(14.5 \times 3.5) - (8.1 + 19.7) = \boxed{}$

5

TOTAL MARKS   15

2D shapes

Triangles

Look at the properties of these different triangles:

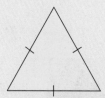   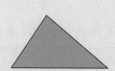

Equilateral	**Isosceles**	**Right-angled**	**Scalene**
3 equal sides. 3 equal angles of 60°. 3 lines of **symmetry**.	2 equal sides. 2 equal angles. 1 line of symmetry.	One angle is a right angle, 90°.	No equal sides. No equal angles.

Quadrilaterals

These are some special four-sided shapes. Look carefully at their properties to sort out similarities and differences.

Square	**Rectangle**	**Rhombus**
4 equal sides. 4 equal angles of 90°. Opposite sides **parallel**. 4 lines of symmetry.	2 pairs of equal sides. 4 equal angles of 90°. Opposite sides parallel. 2 lines of symmetry.	4 equal sides. Opposite angles equal. Opposite sides parallel.

Parallelogram	**Kite**	**Trapezium**
Opposite sides are equal and parallel.	Two pairs of **adjacent** sides are equal.	One pair of parallel sides.

 Some shapes have no lines of symmetry and others have more than one line of symmetry. Try to picture the 'fold lines' on a shape that would fold it exactly in half and count the number of different ways it can be folded in half.

 Key words   symmetry   parallel   adjacent

Triangles

Circle *always*, *sometimes* or *never* for each of these statements.

1   A triangle has 3 acute angles.   always   sometimes   never

2   A triangle has 2 obtuse angles.   always   sometimes   never

3   A triangle has 2 perpendicular sides.   always   sometimes   never

4   A triangle has 2 parallel sides.   always   sometimes   never

5   An isosceles triangle has an obtuse angle.   always   sometimes   never

6   An equilateral triangle has 3 lines of symmetry. always   sometimes   never

6

Quadrilaterals

1   Laura's dictionary gives this definition for a parallelogram:
    'A parallelogram is a quadrilateral that has two pairs of parallel sides.'
    Using this definition, tick each parallelogram for one mark each:

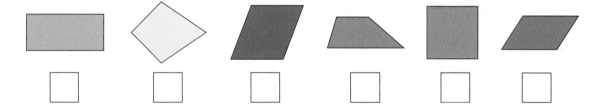

☐   ☐   ☐   ☐   ☐   ☐

2   Write the letter which represents each of these shapes in the correct part of
    this Carroll diagram.

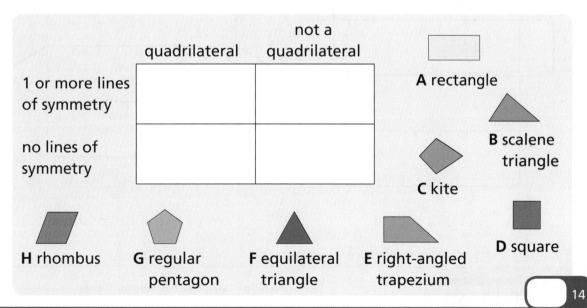

	quadrilateral	not a quadrilateral
1 or more lines of symmetry		
no lines of symmetry		

 A rectangle

B scalene triangle

C kite

D square

H rhombus   G regular pentagon   F equilateral triangle   E right-angled trapezium

14

TOTAL MARKS   20

3D shapes

Parts of 3D shapes

3D shapes are made up of **faces**, **edges** and **vertices** (or corners).

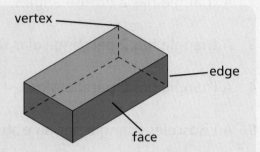

A face is a surface of a solid.

An edge is where two faces meet.

A vertex is where three or more edges meet.

A cuboid has 6 faces, 12 edges and 8 vertices.

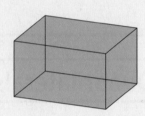

 There is a relationship between the number of faces, edges and vertices of shapes. Euler wrote it as a formula:
Number of Faces + Number of Vertices − Number of Edges = 2
Test the formula F + V − N = 2 on different 3D shapes.

Nets of solids

The **net** of a shape is what it looks like when it is opened out flat. Carefully pull open a cereal box so that it is one large piece of cardboard – this is the net of the box.

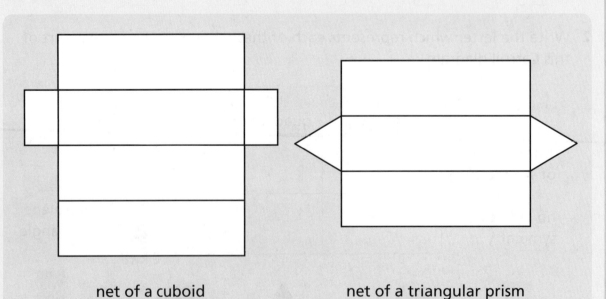

net of a cuboid   net of a triangular prism

Key words   face   edge   vertex/vertices   net

Parts of 3D shapes

Match each description to the shape it describes to complete the sentence.

1	A triangular prism has...	4 triangular faces.
2	A cube has...	2 hexagonal faces and 6 rectangular faces.
3	A tetrahedron has...	2 triangular faces and 3 rectangular faces.
4	A hexagonal prism has...	4 rectangular faces and 2 square faces.
5	A square-based pyramid has...	6 square faces.
6	A cuboid has...	1 square face and 4 triangular faces.

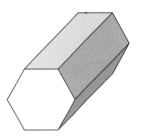

6

Nets of solids

Write the name of each of these shapes from its net.

1 _____

2  _____

3 _____

4 _____

5  _____

6 _____

6

TOTAL MARKS 12

Movement geometry

Moving shapes

A shape can be moved by:

Rotation: a shape can be rotated about a point, clockwise or anticlockwise.

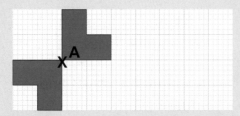

Shape A is rotated 180° around point X.

Reflection: this is sometimes called flipping over.

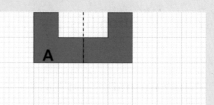

Shape A is reflected. The dotted line is a line of reflection.

Translation: this is sliding a shape across, up, down or diagonally, without rotating or flipping over.

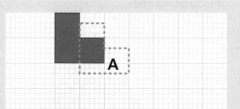

Shape A has moved 5 squares across and 2 squares down.

Rotational symmetry

If you can turn or rotate a shape and fit it onto itself in a different position to the original, then it has rotational **symmetry**. The red dots show the centre of rotation.

The order of rotational symmetry is the number of times the shape can turn to fit onto itself until it comes back to the original position.
Every shape has an order of rotational symmetry of at least 1, so just count the shapes with an order of 2, 3, 4 or more.

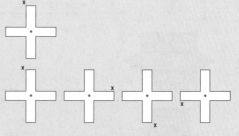

This cross has an order of rotational symmetry of 4.

 Key words   clockwise   anticlockwise   symmetry

Moving shapes

Write whether these shapes have been translated, rotated or reflected.

1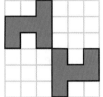

2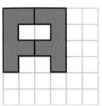

3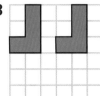

_____   _____   _____

This tile is used to make a pattern.

4 Has this tile been rotated, translated or reflected to make this pattern?

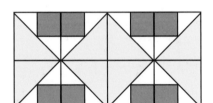

5 Use the tile to draw a different pattern. Is it a translation, rotation or reflection?

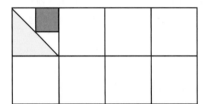

_____   _____   ☐ 5

Rotational symmetry

A square has 4 lines of symmetry and it has an order of rotational symmetry of 4. The letter A is written on the grid below to show this. Write the letter of each shape in the correct space on the grid.

		Number of lines of symmetry				
		0	1	2	3	4
Order of rotational symmetry	1					
	2					
	3					
	4					A

Top Tip *Use a mirror to check lines of symmetry, and tracing paper to work out the order of rotational symmetry of shapes.*

☐ 4

TOTAL MARKS ☐ 9

Coordinates

Positions on a grid

Coordinates are used to show the exact position of a point on a grid.

Two numbers from the x **axis** and the y axis, which could include negative numbers, show the position.

The coordinates of A are (–4,1).

The coordinates of B are (1,2).

The coordinates of C are (4,–3).

Coordinates are always written in brackets and separated by a comma.

This grid has 4 **quadrants**, with negative numbers on the x axis and the y axis.

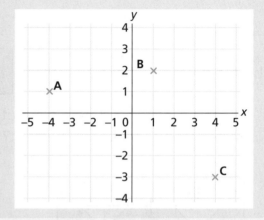

 Top Tip *The numbers on the horizontal x axis are written first, then the vertical y axis. You can remember this because x comes before y and x is a cross!*

Shapes and coordinates

Coordinates are very useful for plotting the vertices of shapes.

Here are two sides of a square.

• What are the coordinates of the three vertices?

• Mark the missing coordinates for the fourth vertex and complete the square.

Remember to read the numbers across and then up for each position.

Draw in the missing lines, using a ruler to make it as accurate as possible.

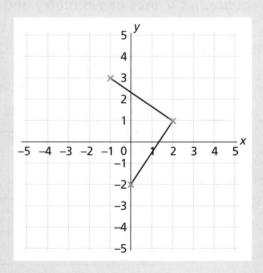

 Key words   axis   horizontal   vertical   quadrant

Positions on a grid

Translate this shape so that it is 4 squares across to the right and 2 squares down. Draw the new shape.

1

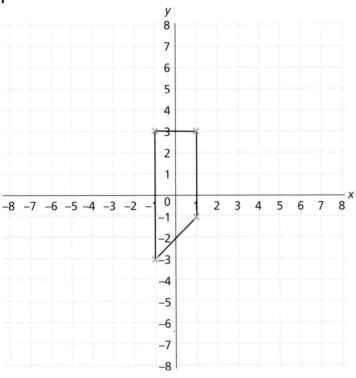

What are the coordinates of the vertices of your translated shape?

2 (⬚ , ⬚), (⬚ ,), (, ⬚), (⬚ , ⬚)

2

Shapes and coordinates

1 This is an isosceles triangle. What is the missing coordinate?

(⬚ , ⬚)

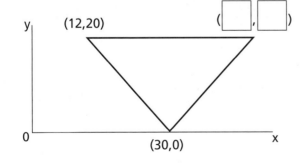

2 This is a rectangle. What is the missing coordinate?

(⬚ , ⬚)

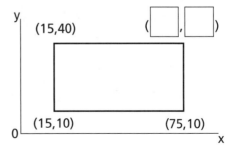

2

TOTAL MARKS [ ] 4

Lines and angles

LEARN

UNDERSTANDING SHAPE

Measuring angles

A **protractor** is used to measure the degree of an angle. It is a good idea to estimate the angle first and then measure it.

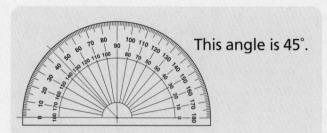

This angle is 45°.

Read from the 0° on the outer scale.

Place the cross at the point of the angle you are measuring.

Angles and shapes

All the angles of a triangle add up to 180°.

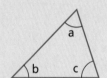

a + b + c = 180°

All the angles of a quadrilateral add up to 360°.

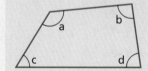

a + b + c + d = 360°

To find the value of missing angles on a triangle, find the total of the angles given and take it away from 180°.

35° + 90° = 125°
180° − 125° = 55°
The missing angle is 55°.

Angles and lines

Angles on a straight line add up to 180°.

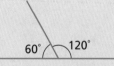

Angles at a point add up to 360°.

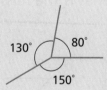

Perpendicular lines meet or cross at 90°.

When two lines cross, the opposite angles are equal.

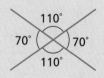

Key words   protractor   perpendicular

Measuring angles

One angle of this quadrilateral is 38°.
Measure the other three angles
accurately using a protractor.

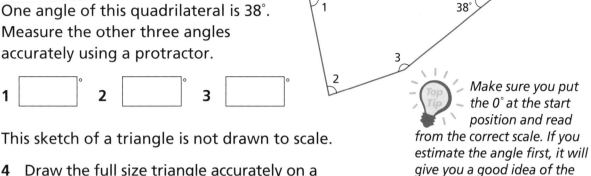

1 [   ]°   **2** [   ]°   **3** [   ]°

Make sure you put the 0° at the start position and read from the correct scale. If you estimate the angle first, it will give you a good idea of the scale you should be reading.

This sketch of a triangle is not drawn to scale.

4 Draw the full size triangle accurately on a
piece of paper. Use a protractor and a ruler.

5 Measure the size of the other two angles.

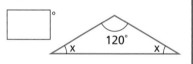

a = [   ]°   b = [   ]°

[5]

Angles and shapes

Do not use a protractor for these questions.

1 Calculate the size of angle x on this isosceles triangle. [   ]°

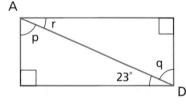

2 Rectangle ABCD has a diagonal line AD.
Calculate the size of angles p, q and r.

p = [   ]°   q = [   ]°   r = [   ]°

[2]

Angles and lines

Calculate the missing angles. Do not use a protractor.

1 [   ]°

38°

2 [   ]°
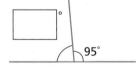
95°

3
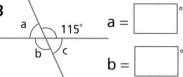
a   115°
b   c

a = [   ]°
b = [   ]°
c = [   ]°

4
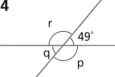
r
49°
q   p

p = [   ]°
q = [   ]°
r = [   ]°

5
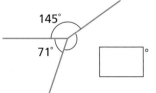
145°
71°
[   ]°

[5]

TOTAL MARKS [   ] 12

Measures

Units of measure

Length, weight (or mass) and capacity are all measured using different units.

Length

1 centimetre (cm) = 10 millimetres (mm)
1 metre (m) = 100 centimetres (cm)
1 kilometre (km) = 1000 metres (m)

Weight

1 kilogram (kg) = 1000 grams (g)
1 tonne = 1000kg

Capacity

1 litre (l) = 1000 millilitres (ml)
1 centilitre (cl) = 100ml

It is important to write the units in your answers and remember that different units can be used for equivalent amounts.

This mirror is 1.825m or 1825mm high.

This bottle holds 2.855 litres or 2855 millilitres.

This feather weighs 0.064kg or 64g.

Imperial measures

We still sometimes use imperial units, which are measures that were used in the past. Try to learn these approximate metric values:

Length

12 inches = 1 foot
2.5cm ≈ 1 inch
30cm ≈ 1 foot
3 feet ≈ 1 metre
5 miles ≈ 8km

Weight

16 ounces = 1 pound (lb)
25g ≈ 1 ounce
2.25lb ≈ 1kg

Capacity

8 pints = 1 gallon
1.75 pints ≈ 1 litre
4.5 litres ≈ 1 gallon

Top Tip
Remember that ≈ means "is approximately equal to".

Key words   equivalent

Units of measure

1 A jug holds 3.5 litres of fruit juice. How many 125ml cupfuls will this fill?

2 There is 40g of sauce in 1 bag. How many bags are there in a 2kg pack?

3 A packet contains 2.7kg of rabbit food. Sam feeds his rabbit with 90g of feed each day. How many days does the packet of feed last?

4 During an athletics training session, Jenny runs 12 laps of a 400-metre track. She wants to run a total of 6km. How many more laps does she need to run?

Write the amounts shown for each of these.

5

6

7

7

PRACTISE

MEASURING

Imperial measures

Underline the best answers for each of these.

1 A man is 6 feet tall. Approximately how many metres is this?

0.4m   1.2m   1.5m   1.8m   2.5m

2 Approximately how many pints are there in 5 litres?

4 pints   7 pints   9 pints   11 pints   15 pints

3 Approximately how many kilometres are there in 6 miles?

2km   5km   8km   10km   18km

4 George catches a 9-pound fish. What is the approximate weight of the fish in kilograms?

1kg   4kg   6kg   7kg   10kg

4

TOTAL MARKS 11

47

Area

Area of rectangles

The area of a shape is the amount of surface that it covers. You can often measure the area of shapes by counting squares. The area of a rectangle can be found without counting if you know the length and width.

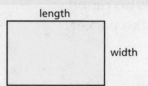

The area is length x width.

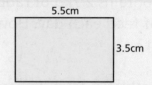

Area = 5.5cm x 3.5cm = 19.25cm^2

 Top Tip *Area is usually measured in square centimetres or square metres, written as cm^2 and m^2. Always remember to write this at the end of the measurement.*

Area of right-angled triangles

Look at this right-angled triangle. It is half a rectangle.

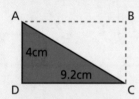

The area of the rectangle ABCD is 4cm × 9.2cm = 36.8cm^2.

The area of the right-angled triangle ACD is half the area of the rectangle ABCD.

$\frac{1}{2}$ of 36.8cm = 18.4cm^2.

The area of a right-angled triangle is: $\frac{1}{2}$ (area of the rectangle)

or

$\frac{1}{2}$ (base × height).

Composite shapes

You might be asked to find the area of a shape that is made up from different rectangles or triangles joined together. Just find the area of each part and then add them together.

Area of rectangle is 4.8cm × 2cm = 9.6cm^2.

Area of square is 2.5cm × 2.5cm = 6.25cm^2.

Total area = 15.85cm^2.

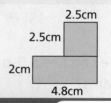

🔑 **Key words**   area

Area of rectangles

Calculate the area of each of these gardens.

1

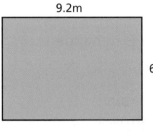

9.2m

6.8m

☐ m²

2

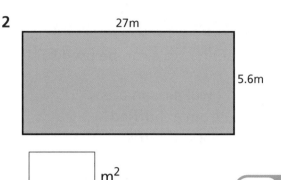

27m

5.6m

☐ m²

2

Area of right-angled triangles

On the grid, draw triangles with the same area as each coloured rectangle. Use a ruler.

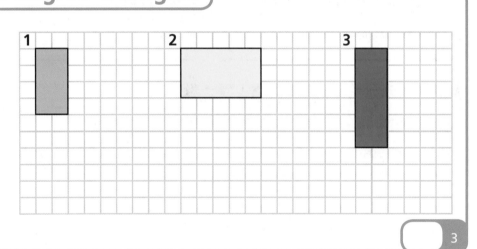

3

Composite shapes

1 On this grid, draw 3 more lines to make a parallelogram with an area of 12 squares.

2 A star is made from this square and four triangles. What is the total area of the star?

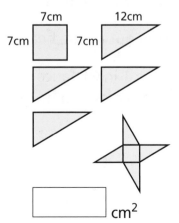

7cm

7cm

12cm

7cm

☐ cm²

3 What is the area of the garden that is grass?

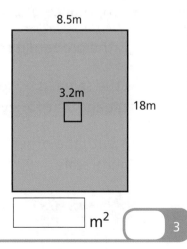

8.5m

3.2m

18m

☐ m²

3

TOTAL MARKS ☐ 8

Probability

The probability scale

A **probability scale** can be used to show how likely an event is to happen:

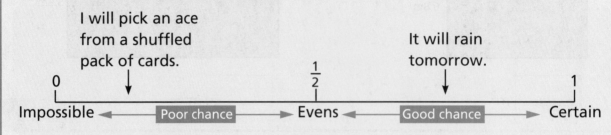

I will pick an ace from a shuffled pack of cards.

It will rain tomorrow.

0 — Impossible ← Poor chance → Evens ← Good chance → 1 — Certain

$\frac{1}{2}$

Top Tip

Remember: 0 is impossible – there needs to be absolutely no chance of it happening, and 1 is certain – it will absolutely, definitely happen. Most events lie somewhere in between these two extremes.

Equally likely outcomes

With activities involving 'chance', such as dice, playing cards, coin tossing or spinners, we can use probability to decide on the possible or likely outcomes.

Even chance is an equal chance of something happening as not happening. We also say a 1 in 2 chance or a 50:50 chance.

Tossing a coin – there is an even chance of it landing on heads.

Rolling a dice – there is an even chance that it will land on an odd number.

Look at this bag of beads. What is the probability of picking out a red bead?

There are 12 beads and 6 of them are red.

$\frac{6}{12}$ is the same as $\frac{1}{2}$, so there is a 1 in 2, or even, chance of picking out a red bead.

What is the probability of picking out a blue bead?

$\frac{6}{12}$ is the same as $\frac{1}{2}$, so there is a 1 in 6 chance. In theory, this means that for every 6 beads picked out, 1 would be blue.

Try this with the other coloured beads and estimate where these lie on the probability scale.

Key words   probability scale   even chance

The probability scale

Where do you think these statements will be on the probability scale?
Join each of them to a position on the scale.

1 When you roll a 1–6 dice, it will show an odd number.

2 Tomorrow will be Monday.

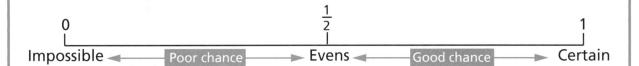

0       $\frac{1}{2}$ 1

Impossible ← Poor chance → Evens ← Good chance → Certain

3 A tulip will grow with no water.

4 Dropped toast will land butter side down.

5 You will have something to drink during the next week.

☐ 5

Equally likely outcomes

1 On a 1–6 dice, what is the probability of throwing…

1      $\frac{1}{3}$ $\frac{1}{2}$ $\frac{1}{6}$ 0

a a six? ☐

d a number greater than 7? ☐

b an even number? ☐

e a number between 0 and 7? ☐

c a number smaller than 3? ☐

Here are two spinners.

Spinner A   **Spinner B**

2 Why is it more likely that you would spin a 5 using Spinner **A** than Spinner **B**?

_____

3 Why are you equally likely to spin an odd number on both spinners?

_____

☐ 7

TOTAL MARKS ☐ 12

Handling data

Frequency charts and grouped data

The word frequency just means 'how many', so a frequency chart is a record of how many of something there are in a group. Frequency charts with grouped data are useful for comparing large groups of numbers.

An airport wanted to compare the weights of the luggage put onto a plane. There were over 180 bags in the survey and they all varied in weight slightly. A graph showing the individual weights would be unhelpful, so it was better to group the data to compare them.

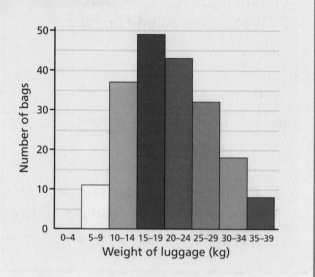

So the most common weight of luggage is between 15kg and 19kg.

Time/distance graphs

Time/distance graphs are exactly what they say – they look at the time taken for each part of a journey.

This is a record of a car journey lasting 4 hours.

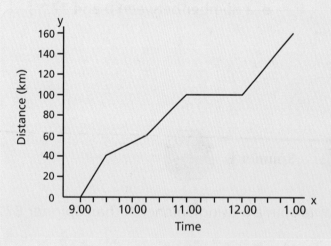

Speed is shown by kilometres per hour (km/h) or miles per hour (mph) – so this is a speed graph. The car travelled 160km in 4 hours, which is an average speed of 40km/h.

Top Tip
The steeper the line, the faster the journey – the car is travelling a greater distance over less time. The horizontal line shows that no distance was travelled for 1 hour.

Key words   frequency

Frequency charts and grouped data

Look at the grouped frequency chart on the opposite page to answer these questions.

1 How many bags weighed between 20kg and 24kg?

2 How many bags weighed less than 20kg?

3 How many bags weighed 30kg or more?

4 Read this statement: 'More bags weighed 30kg or more,
   than weighed 12kg or less.' Tick one of the boxes:

   This is true. ☐   This is false. ☐   Not enough information to say. ☐

5 Read this statement: 'An extra fee is paid on bags weighing 20kg or more.
   Over 50% of the bags have the extra fee to pay.' Tick one of the boxes:

   This is true. ☐   This is false. ☐   Not enough information to say. ☐

5

Time/distance graphs

This is a record of a coach journey.

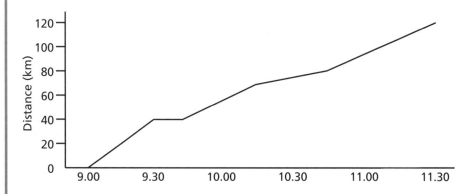

1 At what time did the coach reach its first stop? _____

2 How far did the coach travel between 9.45 and 10.45? _____

3 At approximately what time had the coach travelled 50km? _____

4 How far did the coach travel between 9.30 and 9.45? _____

5 The average speed of the journey was _____ km/h.

5

TOTAL MARKS 10

Mode, median and mean

Mode

The **mode** of a set of data is the number that occurs most often.

These are the maths test scores out of 20 for a group of children:

18   16   14   18   12   13   17   12   16   16   15   11

The modal average for these scores is 16 – there are more of this score than any other. So it is an average because it is more common than any other one.

Median

The **median** is the middle number in a set of numbers.

This chart shows the number of letters received each day for a week.

Monday	Tuesday	Wednesday	Thursday	Friday	Saturday	Sunday
5 letters	4 letters	8 letters	5 letters	3 letters	4 letters	1 letter

To work out the median number of letters, follow these two steps:

1   Put the numbers in order, from smallest to largest: 1, 3, 4, 4, 5, 5, 8.

2   Go to the middle number. 1, 3, 4, **4**, 5, 5, 8. So the median is 4 letters.

When working out the median for an even amount of numbers, you take the two middle numbers, add them together and divide by two.

Mean

The **mean** average is the total ÷ the number of items.

This table shows the number of bikes sold from a shop over 4 weeks.

Mean = total ÷ number of items.

9 + 14 + 18 + 23 = 64   64 ÷ 4 = 16

Week 1	Week 2	Week 3	Week 4
9	14	18	23

So the mean average number of bikes sold is 16.

Top Tip
The range tells us how much the information is spread. To find the range, take the smallest from the largest amount.

Key words   mode   median   mean

Mode

Find the mode for each of the following sets of numbers.

1 17   24   23   24   17   24   16   24   23   Mode: [   ]

2 9.2cm   8.9cm   9.5cm   8.9cm   9.2cm   9.5cm   9.2cm   Mode: [   ] cm

3 32kg   25kg   32kg   51kg   27kg   38kg   32kg   26kg   Mode: [   ] kg

4 108   108   106   101   102   106   101   106   Mode: [   ]

[4]

Median

Find the median for each of the following sets of numbers.

1 34   38   26   29   45   32   34   26   40   Median: [   ]

2 230   234   230   228   230   239   241   Median: [   ]

3 320g   345g   318g   344g   320g   395g   322g   Median: [   ] g

4 6.8m   7.2m   6m   8.8m   6.4m   7.2m   Median: [   ] m

 Top Tip *Rearrange the numbers and list them in order of size to help work out any type of average.*

[4]

Mean

Find the mean for each of the following sets of numbers.

1 37   42   20   32   37   36   Mean: [   ]

2 0.8   0.55   0.3   0.9   0.45   Mean: [   ]

3 9cm   3cm   6cm   8cm   4cm   8cm   6cm   6cm   Mean: [   ] cm

4 300ml   250ml   700ml   450ml   900ml   Mean: [   ] ml

5 8.4km   8.2km   8.6km   8.4km   8.4km   Mean: [   ] km

[5]

TOTAL MARKS [13]

Pie charts

Interpreting pie charts

Pie charts are circles divided into sections. Each section shows a number of items so that they can be compared. You could be asked to give a fraction, a **percentage** or a number as an answer.

A class library has 60 books. This pie chart shows the three types of books.

What fraction of the books are non-fiction?	**What percentage of the books are poetry?**	**How many books are fiction?**
To answer this, look at the total number of sections and the fraction of them that are non-fiction. 2 out of 5, or $\frac{2}{5}$, of the books are non-fiction books.	$\frac{1}{5}$ of the books are poetry books. Change this to a percentage: $\frac{1}{5} = \frac{20}{100} = 20\%$ So 20% of the books are poetry books.	To answer each of these, you need to know what each section represents. There are 60 books altogether and the pie chart is divided into 5 parts, so each individual section represents 12 books. 2 of the sections are fiction, which means that 24 of the books are fiction books.

■ poetry
■ non-fiction
■ fiction

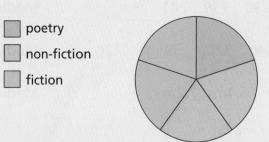

Comparing pie charts

When you compare two pie charts, look carefully at the totals for each and the number of sections.

These pie charts show the results of two hockey teams. Team A played 24 matches and Team B played 18 matches.

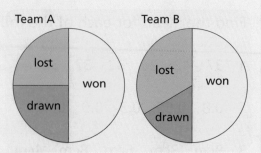

It looks like the two teams have won the same number of matches, but compare them carefully.

Team A have won $\frac{1}{2}$ of 24 matches, which is 12.

Team B have won $\frac{1}{2}$ of 18 matches, which is 9.

Key words | percentage

Interpreting pie charts

Six groups of children built towers from different materials for a problem-solving task.

This pie chart shows the materials used by the six groups to build their towers.

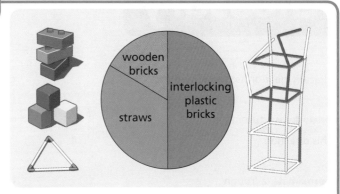

1 Which was the most popular choice of material to build a tower? _____

2 What fraction of the class used wooden bricks? _____

3 How many groups used straws? _____

4 What percentage of the class did **not** use plastic bricks? _____

5 Which type of material did only one group use? _____

5

Comparing pie charts

Tim and Ali bought some material from a DIY shop so they could each build a brick wall.

These pie charts show the material they each bought. Tim spent £140 and Ali spent £160.

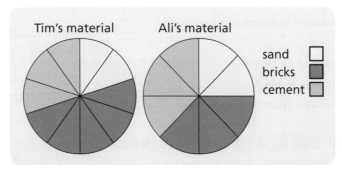

1 What percentage of his money did Tim spend on sand? _____

2 What fraction of his money did Ali spend on cement? _____

3 How much more did Tim spend on bricks than Ali? _____

4 True or false? They both spent the same proportion of their total money on sand. _____

5 Who spent the most money on cement? _____

Top Tip *Always look at the total for the whole 'pie' and then work out what each section is worth by seeing what fraction of the 'pie' it is.*

5

TOTAL MARKS   10

Glossary

adjacent near or next to something

anticlockwise turning in
  this direction

approximate a 'rough'
  answer – near to the real answer

area the area of a shape is the amount of surface that it
  covers

axis (plural is axes) the horizontal or vertical line on a
  graph

clockwise turning in
  this direction

common denominator if two or more fractions have
  the same number as a denominator, then they have a
  common denominator

denominator the bottom number of a fraction, the number
  of parts it is divided into. Example: $\frac{2}{3}$

difference the difference between two numbers is the
  amount by which one number is greater than the other.
  Example: The difference between 18 and 21 is 3

digit there are 10 digits: 0 1 2 3 4 5 6 7 8 and 9 that make
  all the numbers we use

divisor a divisor is a number that another number is
  divided by. Example: for $32 \div 4 = 8$, the divisor is 4

edge where two faces
  of a solid shape meet

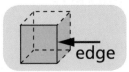

equation where symbols or letters are used instead
  of numbers. Example: $3y = 12$, so $y = 4$

equivalent two numbers or measures are equivalent if
  they are the same or equal

equivalent fraction equivalent fractions are equal
  fractions. Example: $\frac{1}{2} = \frac{2}{4} = \frac{3}{6}$

estimate is like a good guess

even chance if an event has an even chance, there is the
  same chance of it happening as not happening

face the flat side of a
  solid shape

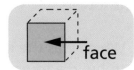

factor a number that will divide exactly into other
  numbers. Example: 5 is a factor of 20

formula a formula (plural is formulae) uses letters or
  words to give a rule

frequency the number of times that something happens
  is called the frequency

highest common factor the greatest whole number that
  divides exactly into two or more other numbers

horizontal a horizontal line is a straight level line across,
  in the same direction as the horizon

lowest common multiple the lowest number that is a
  multiple of two or more numbers

mean this is the total divided by the number of items.
  Example: the mean of 3, 1, 6 and 2 is $(3 + 1 + 6 + 2) \div 4 = 3$

median the middle number in an ordered list. Example: 3, 8,
  11, 15, 16. The median number is 11

mode the most common number in a list. Example: 2, 6,
  4, 2, 5, 5, 2. The mode is 2

multiple a multiple is a number made by multiplying
  together two other numbers

negative number a number less than zero on the number
  line

net the net of a 3D shape is what it looks like when it is
  opened out flat

numerator the top number of a fraction. Example: $\frac{3}{5}$

parallel lines that are parallel always stay the same distance apart and never meet

partition break numbers up into their place values. Example: $476 = 400 + 70 + 6$

percentage this is a fraction out of 100, shown with a % sign

perpendicular a perpendicular line is one that is at right angles to another line

prime factor any factor that is a prime number is a prime factor

prime number a prime number only has two factors, 1 and itself. For example, 23 is a prime number as it can only be divided exactly by 1 and 23

probability scale an ordered line numbered from 0, which is the probability of an impossible event, to 1, which is the probability of a certain event. All probabilities lie between 0 and 1

proportion this is the same as finding the fraction of the whole amount. Example: the proportion of red cubes is 3 out of 5, or $\frac{3}{5}$

protractor a tool for measuring angles

quadrant one quarter of a circle. Also the name given to each of the four quarters on a coordinates grid or graph

quotient this is the number of times that one number will divide into another number. Example: when you divide 18 by 3, the quotient is 6

ratio this compares one amount with another. Example: the ratio of red cubes to blue cubes is 3:2

remainder if a number cannot be divided exactly by another number, then there is a whole number answer with an amount left over, called a remainder

sequence a list of numbers which usually have a pattern. They are often numbers written in order

square number numbers multiplied by themselves make square numbers. Example: $4 \times 4 = 16$. The first five square numbers are 1, 4, 9, 16 and 25

square root the opposite of a square number. A number, when multiplied by itself, makes a square number. Example: the square root of 25 is 5

symmetry when two halves of a shape or pattern are identical

vertical a line that is straight up or down, at right angles to a horizontal line

vertices (single is vertex) the corners of a 3D shape, where edges meet

vertex

Speaking and listening skills

Planning for talking

Whether you have been asked to make a presentation on a topic, or take part in a debate, you need to plan what you want to say and think about how you will present your ideas.

Organise your information in a sensible order, then jot down notes to prompt you when you talk. Using prompts sounds more natural than reading the whole thing out like a script.

Practise speaking aloud, to make sure you are speaking slowly and loudly enough.

Top Tip

Think about the questions you might be asked by the audience and plan how you will respond.

Debating

Debating is all about listening to the views of others and putting your own views across. You may be asked to argue in favour of, or against, a particular idea.

Listen carefully to what people say and jot down anything you disagree with, so you can talk about it when it is your turn to speak. Good debaters reply concisely to the views of their opponents, so that the audience will feel that they have the stronger argument.

Opinions

We all have our own opinions and quite often we form them by listening to what other people say. When someone is speaking, think about whether you agree. Does what they say confirm your opinion, or make you change your mind?

When it is your turn to speak, think about what you could say to convince your listeners to change their opinion.

 Key words | opinion

Planning for talking

Think about your speaking and listening skills. Rate your performance in the following areas by underlining the best option.

1 I speak too quickly.   always   sometimes   <u>never</u>

2 I speak too quietly.   always   <u>sometimes</u>   never

3 I have lots of good opinions.   always   <u>sometimes</u>   never

4 I don't speak out when other
   people are talking.   always   sometimes   <u>never</u>

4

Debating

Imagine you have been asked to debate this question: should children be allowed to cycle to school? List three ideas you could use in favour of the idea.

1 _____

2 _____

3 _____

3

Opinions

Read these quotes. Write a sentence about whether or not you agree and why.

1 "It's cruel to make animals perform in a circus."

I agree because Animals should have freedom not be put to work.

2 "Children watch too much TV."

_____

3 "School children should be allowed to eat whatever they like at lunchtime."

_____

3

The language of books

The features of books

The features of books are all designed to help you to choose and use books.

Feature	Where is it?	What is it for?
Name of the author	On the cover and inside.	Tells readers who wrote the book.
Name of the publisher	On the cover and inside.	Says the name of the company who made and marketed the book.
ISBN	On the back cover.	Allows shops and libraries to identify the book.
Glossary	At the back of the book.	Alphabetical list of technical words and their definitions.
The blurb	On the back cover.	Gives a glimpse of what is inside the book to attract the reader.

The choices publishers make

All of the features you find in books are put there deliberately by authors and publishers to help the book appeal to the audience it has been written for.

For example, the information books you read might have a glossary to help you with new words. They may have information presented in boxes or bullet points to make it easy to read.

Adult non-fiction books are likely to have a lot more content and use more specialist words.

Top Tip

If you are asked to say why you think a piece of text has certain features, remember that they have been put there on purpose, either to attract readers or to help them to read the text.

Key words   author   ISBN   glossary   blurb

The features of books

Fill in the gaps to complete this piece of writing about the features of books.

The covers of books include the name of the writer, or _____,
of the book as well as the name of the publisher. The back carries the
_____, which is the book's unique identifying number.
Inside, the _____ lists the chapters or sections in the book,
while the index lists the topics alphabetically to help readers find what
they need. The _____ lists useful or difficult words and is
found at the back of some books.

4

The choices publishers make

1   Write a sentence to explain why a publisher might present some information
    as bullet points.

    _____

    _____

2   Write a sentence to explain why some information is presented in boxes.

    _____

    _____

3   Why do writers and publishers sometimes include a glossary in non-fiction
    books?

    _____

    _____

3

Fiction and non-fiction

Reading fiction

Fiction authors use their imagination to tell made-up stories, although they could be based on a real person or an event that actually happened.

Fiction for older children and adults is not usually illustrated. Instead, the author uses detailed description and special techniques to create a picture for the reader.

> The chilly wind ran icy fingers through bare winter branches.

When you are reading fiction, especially in a test, look out for how the writer uses these techniques and be ready to comment on how they build up a picture.

Top Tip

You will find out about different creative writing techniques and how to use them later in the book.

Reading non-fiction

Non-fiction writing is designed to give information and is packed full of facts. Information is organised into chapters and sections, so readers can find what they need without reading the whole book.

Books are often split into chapters on different subjects. Topics are also listed alphabetically in the index, so readers know exactly where to look.

Non-fiction is often richly illustrated, with pictures, photographs, charts and diagrams all helping to explain the information. Sections of text may be presented as bullet points or put into separate boxes to make it quicker and easier to read.

In a test, think about what kind of non-fiction writing you are reading and make a note of how the information is organised on the page. How does this help the reader?

Key words   fiction   non-fiction

Reading fiction

Choose a fiction book that you have read. Find a sentence in which the author has used descriptive language to help you to imagine
what a person or place looks like. Copy it out neatly here.

_____

_____

_____

_____

1

Reading non-fiction

Now have a look at a non-fiction book. Tick each of these features when you find them.

A picture caption, to explain what is in a picture. ☐

A photograph. ☐

Information presented in bullet points. ☐

Information in a box. ☐

An index. ☐

5

TOTAL MARKS 6

Reading skills

Reading techniques

We need to be able to find information in writing so that we can answer questions in reading comprehension tests.

Skim through the piece of writing quickly to begin with. Think about whether the text is fiction or non-fiction and what it is about. Also, look out for how the text is organised.

Next, read the questions carefully and think about what information you need to answer them. **Scan** through the text again to find key words like the name of a person or place, or a date.

Some questions ask for your opinion. They might ask you what you think about a subject, or what you think the writer feels. You need to read the text carefully again and always back up your answer with evidence.

Top Tip *If you need to find a date or name, make sure you have found the right one, as there may be more than one!*

Using deduction

Sometimes, the answer to a question might not be obvious at first. You might need to read the text again really carefully and think hard about the question. Looking for clues like this is called **deduction**. Also try to imagine how you would feel if you were a character in the story, or the writer of the text. This is called **empathy**.

When you think you have the answer, make sure you back up your opinion with evidence from the text.

Key words   skim   scan   deduction   empathy

Reading techniques

Use your reading skills to answer the questions about this piece of writing.

Holidaymakers visiting Seaward this summer will be surprised to find their view of the beachfront obscured by the latest 'improvement' to the town centre. The new 10-screen cinema opened in March and has, since then, shown films on fewer than half of its screens. Despite its apparent lack of success, the venue's customers have caused traffic chaos on several occasions and one can only imagine how much worse it will be in peak season. Those of us who remember Seaward as a tasteful, sleepy resort are less than impressed.

1   Is the writing fiction or non-fiction? _____

2   What is it about? _____

    _____

3   What is the name of the town? _____

4   Why does the writer think that the traffic chaos will be worse in peak season?

    _____

    _____

4

Using deduction

Read the text again and answer these questions.

1   Do you think the writer is young or old? Explain your answer.

    _____

2   Suggest one reason for the writer's opinion on the new development. Provide evidence for your idea from the text.

    _____

    _____

2

TOTAL MARKS 6

Authors and narrators

Authors

Authors are writers. Fiction authors often have their own personal style. Some often write about similar topics, like animal stories or action adventures. Others write on a variety of topics but use a similar format such as diary entries.

If you really enjoy a book, find out if the author has written any others.

If you find an author whose books you love, make sure you tell your friends!

I love Anthony Horowitz!

Jacqueline Wilson is great!

Top Tip

Your local library will be able to find out about books an author has written and get hold of copies for you to read.

Narrator and viewpoint

The storyteller in a piece of fiction is called the narrator and we read things from their viewpoint.

Narrators who are not part of the story can tell the reader things that none of the characters know. This can help to build suspense because the reader waits to find out how the characters will react to unfolding events.

When the narrator is a character in the story, the reader gets to know them really well and will be keen to find out what happens to them.

When they choose their narrator, authors also think about how much they want their reader to know at various points in the story.

For example, we know that Cinderella is the beautiful woman at the ball long before the prince does. If the prince were the narrator, we wouldn't know very much about her until he slips the glass slipper onto her foot. How would this affect the story?

Key words   narrator   viewpoint

Authors

1 Think about two books that you have read that are written by the same author. Write down two things that are similar about them. Are they about similar subjects? Are they for the same age group? Are the stories similar in a different way?

a _____

_____

b _____

_____

2 Which book did you prefer? Give a reason for your answer.

_____

_____

3

Narrator and viewpoint

Think again about the well-known story of Cinderella. Write a short paragraph of three sentences about the ball, with one of the ugly sisters as the narrator. Remember that the sisters did not know that Cinders was at the ball!

_____

_____

_____

_____

_____

_____

_____

3

TOTAL MARKS   6

Life stories

Biography

A **biography** is the life story of a person that is written by someone else.

Often, biographies are written about historical figures that people today would like to know more about.

Biographies are written in the **third person**. That means the author is writing about the life of someone else and focuses on what he or she does.

> **She** studied art at college before opening **her** own studio.

Biography is non-fiction and writers research their subjects carefully to get the facts right. Even so, the writer will choose which facts to include and which to leave out, so a biography can never give a complete picture of someone's life.

Autobiography

Autobiographies are life stories written by the person whose story they tell. They are written in the **first person**, so the words show that the writer is telling his or her own story.

> **I** hated **my** itchy brown school uniform and dreamed of being able to choose what **I** wore.

Autobiography is non-fiction but because the author chooses which events to write about and which to leave out, it may not give an entirely accurate picture, especially as our recollection of events may change over time.

Top Tip *Using the first person can be very effective because it makes the reader feel that the person they are finding out about is speaking directly to them.*

 Key words | biography   third person   autobiography   first person

Biography

Answer these questions about biographies.

1 Biographies are written in the third person. Why is this?

_____

_____

_____

2 Does a biography give a complete account of someone's life? Explain your answer.

_____

_____

_____

_____

2

Autobiography

1 What effect does using the first person have on readers of autobiographies?

_____

_____

2 Think of someone you admire, whose autobiography you would like to read. Write down **three** things you would like to find out about them from their autobiography.

a _____

b _____

c _____

_____

4

TOTAL MARKS   6

Sentences

Sentence types

A **sentence** is a group of words that work together. Within sentences, **clauses** contain a **verb** and a **subject**. A subject is the person or thing that does the action.

Simple sentences contain one clause.

Sam bought some trainers.

subject   verb

Compound sentences are made when two clauses with equal importance are joined together with a special type of word called a **conjunction**.

Jo let the balloon go and it drifted into the sky.

clause 1   conjunction   clause 2

Complex sentences are built around a **main clause** that would make sense on its own. Added to it is one or more less important clauses, called **subordinate clauses**. They would not make sense on their own.

Joe did his homework while he ate his tea.

main clause   subordinate clause

 Top Tip *Sometimes a subordinate clause is embedded in the middle of a sentence, e.g. My auntie, **who lives in Spain**, sent me a birthday card.*

Using sentence types

When you write, aim to use a variety of sentence types. Too many simple sentences make reading hard work, because the reader must pause every time they reach a full stop. They can be great for drawing attention to important bits in your writing though.

Compound and complex sentences allow you to combine ideas in different ways. The reader does not have to keep pausing for full stops but they have to work out how the two ideas relate to each other and this can slow them down too.

 Key words

sentence	clause	verb	subject	simple sentence
compound sentence	conjunction	complex sentence
main clause	subordinate clause

Sentence types

Decide whether each of these sentences is simple, compound or complex.

1 It is cold tonight.

Simple

2 While Dad was out, we baked his birthday cake.

Complex
~~Compound~~

3 Eve stroked the cat and it purred happily.

Simple
~~Compound~~
~~Simple~~

4 I wanted to buy some shoes but the shop had shut.

Compound

5 We ran for the bus although it had already started moving.

Compound

> **Top Tip**
> In a complex sentence, the subordinate clause sometimes comes at the start.

5

Using sentence types

1 Give an example of how writers can use simple sentences successfully.

_____

_____

2 Write down one good and one bad effect that using compound or complex sentences can have on a reader.

Good _____

_____

Bad _____

_____

3

TOTAL MARKS 8

Contractions

Writing contractions

Contractions happen when two words are joined together, with one or more letters missing. The position of the missing letters is shown by an **apostrophe**.

I am = I'm	she is = she's
he will = he'll	they will = they'll
do not = don't	is not = isn't
I would = I'd	I have = I've

Most contractions are easy to write, but a few are harder. Sometimes letters are missed out in more than one place, or the letters are put in a different order!

will not = won't	shall not = shan't

Using contractions

Contractions happen over time when we use two words together. We use them all the time when we talk to one another, but there are rules about using them in writing.

Contractions are great for bringing your characters' dialogue to life when you are writing stories. Writing **dialogue** the way people really speak makes it much more believable.

isearch
Hi Soph,

Can't wait to see you Sat night.
I've got a fab new dress to wear.
What are you wearing?

Hugs,
Hels x

You can also use them for informal writing, like letters or emails to friends.

Top Tip *Contractions should not be used in formal writing, like schoolwork or formal letters.*

 Key words   contraction   apostrophe   dialogue

Writing contractions

This piece of writing contains **five** incorrectly spelt contractions. Can you underline them?

> Dear Katie,
>
> Hows your new home? We're really missing you at school. Your lucky
>
> though because wer'e doing lots of tests this week. I cant believe it'll
>
> be Christmas soon. You'l have to come and stay over the holidays.
>
> Take care,
>
> Beth

5

Using contractions

The writer of this formal letter has used contractions. Cross them out, then write the full forms in the spaces.

Dear Sirs,

I'm _____ writing to complain about the service we've

_____ received in your Newtown branch. We purchased a

kettle from the branch but when we got home we found that the lid

wasn't _____ in the box. The manager said she'd

_____ replace it but we haven't _____ heard

anything since then.

I would be grateful if you could look into the matter for me.

Yours faithfully,

M Dawson

5

TOTAL MARKS   10

Possessive apostrophes

Using possessive apostrophes

We can use **possessive apostrophes** to say that something belongs to someone or something.

When the person or thing an object belongs to is **singular**, you usually add an apostrophe then *s*.

Sophie's watch   the squirrel's tail

If you are saying that an object belongs to more than one person and the word already ends in *s*, you usually just add an apostrophe without adding another *s*.

two cats' tails   four boys' bags

Some **plural** nouns do not end in *s*. With these, you add an apostrophe, then *s*.

the children's games   the people's hats

Top Tip *Don't forget, you can also use possessive adjectives like* **my**, **his**, **our** *and* **their** *to say that something belongs to someone.*

Its and it's

People often get mixed up between *its* and *it's*. You need to remember that *its* does not have an apostrophe when you are saying that something belongs to *it*.

The flag fluttered on **its** pole.   The bird settled on **its** nest.

It's is the contracted form of *it is*.

It's too late to play.   **It's** hot today.

Key words   possessive apostrophe   singular   plural   adjective

Using possessive apostrophes

Write these sentences again, with the possessive apostrophes in the correct place.

1 The mens cars were parked side by side.

<u>The men's cars were parked side by side</u>

2 The seals enclosure was next to the penguins.

_____

_____

3 The womens suitcases were stacked on a trolley.

_____

4 The two puppies tails waved wildly.

_____

_____

Top Tip *The position of the possessive apostrophe is often the only way a reader can tell whether you are writing about one person, or more than one.*

4

Its and it's

Write two sentences using the word *its* and then two using *it's*.

1 _____

2 _____

3 _____

4 _____

4

Punctuation

Commas

LEARN

WRITING

Commas can be used to separate clauses in sentences. They tell readers when to pause, which helps them to understand the sentence properly.

In this complex sentence, a comma separates the main clause from the subordinate clause.

As she ran over, Katie shouted the exciting news.

Without the comma, it would sound like someone had run over Katie!

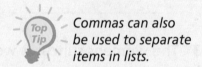

Top Tip — *Commas can also be used to separate items in lists.*

Colons and semi-colons

Colons and **semi-colons** can both be used to organise sentences to make them easier to understand.

Semi-colons are used to separate clauses in sentences. Often they can be used to join two simple sentences together into one sentence.

I called my dog. He came running in.

I called my dog; he came running in.

Colons are used to introduce explanations or lists.

I was late for school. The bus was late.

I was late for school: the bus was late.

Parenthesis

Parenthesis is where words are added to a sentence in brackets to give the reader more information. Where you put the brackets is important. The sentence must make sense whether or not the reader reads the words in brackets.

The girl fell asleep.

The girl (who had been awake since early morning) fell asleep.

Key words   comma   colon   semi-colon   parenthesis

Commas

Add the commas to these sentences.

1 My aunt who lives in Scotland is coming to stay next week.

2 When the film had finished we went out for pizza.

3 Anna Rachel Katie and Ruth sit on my table at school.

4 Yawning tiredly Mark went to bed.

4

Colons and semi-colons

Put a tick by a sentence that you think is true and a cross by one you think is false.

1 Colons can be used at the end of a sentence, instead of a full stop. ✗

2 Colons can be used to introduce lists. ✓

3 Semi-colons can sometimes be used to join two simple sentences. ✓

4 Semi-colons can be used instead of speech marks. ✗

4

Parenthesis

Underline the sentences in which the parenthesis has been used correctly.

1 I forgot my PE kit (again!).

2 My little brother rummaged (who is not allowed in my room) through my things.

3 (It started to rain) as we were walking home.

4 The car (which was very old) ground to a halt at the side of the road.

4

TOTAL MARKS 12

Writing about speech

Direct and reported speech

Reported speech is where the writer tells the reader about what someone has said, without using their exact words.

> The teacher told the class to be quiet.

It can be useful in stories because it allows you to write about what a character says without them having to be in the story at that point.

Direct speech is where the writer uses the actual words that someone says.
Speech marks show that someone is speaking and separates what they say from the rest of the sentence.

> "You're so cute!" whispered Claire.

Direct speech is brilliant for bringing your characters to life and letting them talk to each other.

 Use a combination of direct and reported speech in stories, as too much of either can make reading hard work.

You're so cute!

Using dialogue to develop characters

When characters talk to each other, it is called dialogue. Real people talk all the time, so using dialogue is a brilliant way to develop realistic characters. Think about the kind of person your character is. Are they happy or sad? Kind or nasty? This will affect what they say and how they say it.

> The crazy inventor bounded across the room towards us. "**Hello**!" he **boomed, cheerfully**.

Try to avoid using the word *said* when you are introducing direct speech. Words like *asked, replied, argued* or *suggested* help to say lots more about how a character is speaking.

 Key words   reported speech   direct speech   speech marks

Direct and reported speech

1 Write this sentence again as reported speech.

"Shall we go shopping on Saturday?" suggested Mel.

_____

2 Write this sentence again as direct speech.

Mark explained that he was late because the bus had broken down.

_____

3 Write down one benefit of using direct speech.

_____

4 Write down one benefit of using reported speech.

_____

4

Using dialogue to develop characters

Choose the best ending for these sentences about characters from a story. Underline your choices.

1 "I want it now!"

screamed the spoilt boy, rudely.

whispered the spoilt boy, shyly.

giggled the spoilt boy, excitedly.

2 "Cheer up!"

ordered the little girl, sharply.

shrieked the little girl, angrily.

coaxed the little girl, cheerfully.

2

TOTAL MARKS 6

Nouns and pronouns

Noun types

Nouns are words that name things.

Common nouns name ordinary things, e.g. shop, tree.

Proper nouns name people and places, and things like the days of the week and the months of the year. Proper nouns start with a capital letter wherever they appear in a sentence, e.g. Simon, Cornwall.

Abstract nouns name things that you can't touch or hold, like ideas or feelings, e.g. happiness, knowledge.

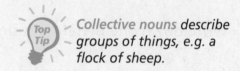
Collective nouns describe groups of things, e.g. a flock of sheep.

Pronouns

Pronouns like *I, me, she, he, they* and *us* can sometimes be used in place of nouns. They can save you from having to use the same noun again and again.

> I tried to open the door, but **it** was stuck.

There are different pronouns to replace different nouns. Some help you to write about yourself, some are for males, some are for females and some are for groups of people.

Pronouns are really useful, but you need to use them with care.

> The puppy chewed the slipper, so Dad threw it away.

Do you think Dad threw away the slipper or the puppy? It is impossible to be sure, because *it* could replace either noun!

Make sure the pronouns give enough information about what is happening in your sentences.

Key words | noun common noun proper noun abstract noun
collective noun pronoun

Noun types

Write down **three** examples of each type of noun, for one mark each.

common noun	proper noun	abstract noun
_____	_____	_____
_____	_____	_____
_____	_____	_____

9

Pronouns

Add a suitable pronoun to complete each sentence.

1 Kathryn and Liz are my friends although _____ live far away.

2 When my baby sister starts crying, I know _____ is tired.

3 Dad ran after the dog but he couldn't catch _____ .

3

Plurals

Spelling rules for plurals

Plural means more than one of a particular noun. Many plurals end in *s*.

shoes   gloves   socks

Singular nouns that end in *ss, sh, ch* or *x* end in *es* in the plural.

stitches   dishes   boxes

If the noun ends in a consonant then *y*, you must change the *y* to *ies*.

babies   ladies   jellies

With nouns that end in a consonant then *f*, you usually change the *f* to *ves*.

leaf   leaves

Top Tip *Words that end in **o** can be tricky. Most end in **es** in the plural, but some just end in **s** and some can have either ending. Check in a dictionary if you are not sure.*

Irregular plurals

Some nouns do not follow the rules when they become plurals. You need to learn these separately.

mouse	mice
child	children
person	people

Others are spelt the same, whether they are singular or plural.

fish   deer   sheep

Key words   plural   singular

Spelling rules for plurals

Match up these word openings with the correct plural ending.

1 fox   es

2 train   eys

3 wol   s

4 pupp   ves

5 donk   ies

6 tomato   es

6

Irregular plurals

Write down the plurals of these nouns.

1 species   _____

2 man   _____

3 antelope   _____

4 ox   _____

5 woodlouse   _____

6 tooth   _____

6

TOTAL MARKS   12

Adjectives

Using adjectives

Adjectives describe nouns. Adjectives can help you to describe exactly what something is like. They can describe the size, shape and colour of something, how many there are, and who they belong to.

Try to avoid tired adjectives like *good*, *bad* or *big*, as there are many different ways something can be good, bad or big! Look for really powerful ones instead, that say more about the thing you are describing.

Huge, black clouds hung in the **gloomy** sky.

Comparative and superlative adjectives

Comparative adjectives allow you to compare two things.

My dog is **bigger** than yours.

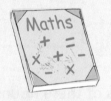

My maths homework is **more difficult** than my English work.

Superlative adjectives describe the most of a particular quality something can be.

My dog is the **biggest** of all.   It was the **most exciting** film I have ever seen.

 *Superlative adjectives are often used in persuasive writing, like adverts, e.g. the **latest** development in gaming.*

🔑 **Key words**   adjective   comparative adjective   superlative adjective

Using adjectives

Write these sentences again, with more powerful adjectives replacing the bold words.

1 A **small** bird sat on the **old** fence.

A tiny Bird sat on the Ancient Fence

2 The **kind** girl gave her friend a **nice** present.

The genours girl gave her friend an Amazing present.

3 A **big** storm blew **cold** rain into our faces.

A bellowing Storm blew freezing rain onto our faces.

4 I was **tired** at the end of the race but **pleased** that I had won.

I Was exausted at the end of the race but

proud that I had won

8

Comparative and superlative adjectives

Fill in this chart with the missing words.

	Comparative adjectives	Superlative adjectives
funny		funniest
flat	flatter	
pretty		
expensive		least expensive
exciting	more exciting	
generous		

Top
Tip

When you add the **er** suffix to words, you often have to change the spelling of the root word first.

8

TOTAL MARKS 16

Verbs

Using verbs

Verbs describe actions. Every sentence must have a verb, but that doesn't mean you have to keep using the same ones again and again. Try to pick verbs that describe exactly what a person or thing is doing.

> The cat **walked** up to the bird.   The cat **crept** up to the bird.

Look for interesting verbs, which say more about the action.

> walked ➜ sauntered   said ➜ explained   went ➜ travelled

Verb tenses

Verbs change their tense to tell us whether something has already happened, is happening now, or will happen in the future.

> I swam in a competition. (past tense)
>
> I am swimming in a competition. (present tense)
>
> I shall swim in a competition. (future tense)

Lots of past tense verbs end in *ed*, but many are completely different in the past tense.

> is ➜ was   bring ➜ brought   lose ➜ lost   eat ➜ ate

Active and passive verbs

Verbs can be active or passive.
Active verbs tell us about something   The dog ate its biscuits.
that a person or thing is doing.

Sentences that contain a passive verb tell us about what is being done, but might not always tell us who or what is doing the action.

> The door was slammed shut in my face.

We know what happened to the door, but not who slammed it!

 Key words   tense   past tense   present tense   future tense
active verb   passive verb

Using verbs

Think of three verbs you could use instead of each of these verbs.

1 said   _____   _____   _____

2 went   _____   _____   _____

3 ran   _____   _____   _____

9

Verb tenses

Write these present tense sentences again, in the past tense.

1 Sam buys a newspaper.

_____

2 Kate writes a letter to her friend.

_____

3 Chris and Daniel find a key on the pavement.

_____

 Some verbs stay the same in the present tense and the past tense, e.g. **read, hit, cut, hurt**.

3

Active and passive verbs

Decide whether you think each sentence contains an active or a passive verb. Write A for active or P for passive in each box.

1 The boy was taken to hospital.

2 The baby threw its rattle across the room.

3 The bird caught a worm.

4 The window was suddenly broken.

4

TOTAL MARKS   16

Adverbs

Making adverbs work for you

Adverbs are words that describe verbs.
They allow you to say more about how an action takes place.

The wind blew **gently**.

The wind blew **fiercely**.

Many adverbs end in *ly*. In fact, a lot of
them are made by adding *ly* to an adjective.

silent + ly = silently

Other adverbs have different endings.
Very, here and *there* are all adverbs too.

Teaming up the right adverb with a really
powerful verb can transform your writing.

She walked angrily out of the room.

She stormed furiously out of the room.

Which sentence paints a more vivid picture?

Using adverbs

Verbs can be used without adverbs, but every adverb needs a verb to work with.

Most of the time, the verb comes first, followed by the adverb.

The girls whispered secretively.

verb   adverb

Sometimes, though, adverbs can work really well at the start of a sentence.
This works brilliantly when the way in which an action takes place is the most
important thing in the sentence.

Suddenly, the door burst open.

adverb   verb

Key words   adverb

Making adverbs work for you

Improve each sentence by replacing the blue verb and the green adverb with more interesting alternatives. Write the new sentences.

The teacher spoke nicely to the children.

The teacher chatted kindly to the children.

1 "Who are you?" asked the man, crossly.

_____

2 Max ate the cake quickly.

_____

3 Jane walked slowly in the sunshine.

_____

3

Using adverbs

Write these sentences again, with the red adverb at the beginning.

Sarah greeted her cousin shyly.   Shyly, Sarah greeted her cousin.

1 The knight bravely climbed the castle walls.

_____

2 Gemma carelessly tore the paper off the present.

_____

3 Jake slammed the door furiously.

_____

4 Tom found his football boots eventually.

_____

4

TOTAL MARKS 7

Synonyms

Avoiding repetition

Synonyms are words with similar meanings. We can use them to avoid having to repeat the same word in our writing.

> The cat **walked** along the fence, jumped down and **walked** into the house.

The repetition in this sentence is rather boring. Replacing one or both of the bold words will make it sound better.

> The cat **crept** along the fence, jumped down and **stalked** into the house.

Read your writing through carefully, to see if you need to find synonyms for words you have repeated.

Improving descriptions

Synonyms can also help us to describe things in better detail. This is because not all synonyms have exactly the same meaning. Choosing the correct one for each sentence will make your writing much more interesting to read.

> The squirrel **ran** across the lawn towards the tree and the dog **ran** after it.

In this sentence, both animals are running. Squirrels and dogs run in very different ways though, so replacing the verb 'ran' with carefully chosen synonyms will avoid repetition and give the sentence more meaning.

> The squirrel **scampered** across the lawn towards the tree and the dog **tore** after it.

Top Tip

Synonyms can help you to write great poetry, because you can pick a synonym with the right number of syllables, or one which rhymes with another word.

Key words   synonym   thesaurus

Avoiding repetition

Read this piece of writing through and underline words that you would replace with synonyms, to avoid repetition. Write the new words you would use on the lines below.

It was a hot day and we were soon hot and tired. We were all glad to reach the edge of the woodland and feel the cool woodland floor beneath our feet. As we began to pick a path through the trees, we began to hear the sounds of small creatures creeping through the undergrowth. As we got deeper into the forest, we started to feel afraid. We were afraid we would get lost, then Sam told us he had lost his compass!

1 _____   4 _____

2 _____   5 _____

3 _____

 Top Tip *Many of the words we use most often have synonyms and you can find more in a* **thesaurus***, which lists words alphabetically, along with their synonyms.*

5

Improving descriptions

Choose the best synonym to complete each sentence. Cross out the words you reject.

1 Dad (shattered   smashed   broke) an egg into the cake mixture.

2 The rabbit (jumped   hopped   leapt) happily around its cage.

3 The hairdresser (cut   sliced   chopped) my hair.

4 The woman (laundered   washed   hosed) the little boy's dirty face.

5 Mum and I (embellished   enhanced   decorated) the Christmas tree.

5

TOTAL MARKS   10

Imagery

Writing imagery

Imagery is the name given to creative writing techniques that help to build up a picture for your readers. There are three main types you can use.

Simile is a way of comparing one thing with another, using the words *as* or *like*.

Cherries shone like jewels in the branches of the trees.

Metaphor is where you say that an object is something else.

The mountain was a sleeping giant.

Personification is where a non-human thing is described using human characteristics.

Huge fir trees stood guard by the gate to the castle.

Imagery is perfect for writing really effective fiction, as you can use it to write strong descriptions of the way things look, sound, feel, taste or smell. You would not normally use it in non-fiction writing like reports, recounts, letters or instructions.

> **Top Tip** *If you are asked to write about a piece of text that someone else has written, be sure to comment on how they have used imagery.*

Avoiding clichés

There are lots of well-known similes and metaphors that we use all the time when we are speaking. These are called **clichés**.

as pretty as a picture   a wolf in sheep's clothing

Most people have heard phrases like this lots of times before, so they can sound a bit boring if they are used in writing. Have a go at writing your own imagery instead.

Key words   imagery   simile   metaphor   personification   cliché

Writing imagery

Look at the picture, then answer the questions.

1 Write a sentence containing a simile to describe the weather in the picture.

_____

2 Write a sentence containing a metaphor to describe the house.

_____

3 Write a sentence containing personification to describe the washing on the line.

_____

_____

3

Avoiding clichés

Underline the clichés in these sentences. Then write the sentences again, using your own imagery.

1 The sun smiled down on the village.

_____

2 Our dog is as gentle as a lamb.

_____

3 My science homework is a nightmare.

_____

3

TOTAL MARKS   6

Special effects

Using alliteration and onomatopoeia

Good writers use the way words sound to create powerful effects in their writing.

Alliteration is where words that start with the same sound are used together. When they are read out, the repeated sound helps to draw your reader's attention to that part of the writing.

Looking up, Simon saw a spider on the ceiling.

The rabbit hopped into the wood, followed by the furtive fox.

Onomatopoeia is where words sound like the things they describe.

Frogs **croaked** from the river bank.

The baby **wailed** in its pram.

An onomatopoeic word allows you to describe what something sounds like in a single word.

> *Top Tip*
> *You will need to use your knowledge of synonyms to find words with the right meaning that start with the correct sound.*

Reading alliteration and onomatopoeia

In reading tests, you will often be asked why you think a writer has used a particular phrase. To get full marks, you need to say what type of technique has been used and what effect it creates.

> The writer has used alliteration to emphasise how strong the wind is. Repeating the 'w' sound also draws attention to the whistling sound of the wind.

The wind wailed and whipped through the trees, tearing at the branches. Above the noise of the storm came a cracking sound followed by a scraping, as the shed roof was torn loose and dragged along the garden path.

> The writer has used onomatopoeia to help the reader to imagine the sound of the shed roof blowing off and the damage that has been done.

 Key words   alliteration   onomatopoeia

Using alliteration and onomatopoeia

1 Imagine you are rocking in a rowing boat on a calm sea. Use alliteration to write a sentence describing what it is like.

_____

2 Imagine you are carrying a tray of china cups and plates. You trip and drop the tray. Write a sentence using onomatopoeia to describe the sound it makes.

_____

2

Reading alliteration and onomatopoeia

Read the text, then answer the questions.

> We went to see the tigers next. One of the males padded past, huge paws pounding in the dust. He turned and faced us, baring his sharp teeth and growling.

1 Why has the writer used the phrase _padded past, huge paws pounding_?

_____

2 Why do you think the writer has used the word _growling_?

_____

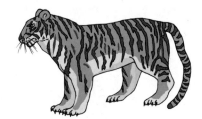

2

TOTAL MARKS   4

Instructions

The language of instructions

Instructions do not ask you to do something, they tell you! They do this by using the **imperative**. That means that they use the verb first, without using a noun or pronoun before it.

> **Draw** around a circular plate.
>
> **Cut** carefully around the circle.

In any other kind of writing, ordering people around like this would seem rude! It works in instructions, however, because it makes the reader focus on what they need to do.

Instructions often contain technical vocabulary and may contain specific information, like numbers, to tell the reader how many or how much of a particular thing the reader needs to use.

> Use a **balloon whisk** to whip **two** egg whites.

It is important to get details like this correct, or the instructions might not work.

Organising instructions

Instructions break a task down into small steps that are described chronologically. It is usually very important that the tasks are carried out in the correct order, so they are often numbered to make sure.

They might also contain time connectives to tell the reader when to do each step.

> **Once** the egg whites are soft and fluffy, fold in the sugar.
>
> Bake in a hot oven **until** the meringue is golden brown.

Top Tip *Using a flow chart to plan instructions will make sure you write the steps in the correct order and don't miss anything out.*

 Key words | imperative

The language of instructions

Write these sentences again, using the imperative to turn them into instructions.

1   You need to allow 7 working days for your order to be processed.

_____

2   You should keep your receipt as proof of purchase.

_____

Underline the technical vocabulary used in these sentences.

3   Cut round your design with a craft knife.

4   Use an adjustable spanner to tighten the bolts.

4

Organising instructions

Think about where you are sitting now. Write four numbered instructions to tell someone else how to get to the nearest door.

1   _____

2   _____

3   _____

4   _____

4

Persuasive writing

Persuasive language

Persuasive writing like adverts and brochures uses powerful language to build up a convincing argument for why the reader should buy a product, visit an attraction or adopt a particular point of view.

Most persuasive writing uses very few words, so each one must work hard to persuade the reader. Adverts often use superlative adjectives to make the product, place or idea sound like the best choice. Powerful adjectives help to create the idea that it is good value, or exciting in some way.

> The highest, fastest white-knuckle ride on the planet.

Persuasive writing often doesn't need to be written in full sentences. Give it a strong title, then use bullet points, boxed text and sub-headings. Don't forget to think about any factual information you need to include, like prices, addresses and dates.

Understanding your reader

The key to successful persuasive writing is to understand the audience you are writing for. You need to build up a convincing argument that will appeal to your reader.

For example, if you were writing a leaflet about a holiday park designed for adults wanting to book a holiday, you would probably emphasise things like value for money and convenience. If the leaflet was for a child, you might write about all the sports on offer and the huge ice cream parlour.

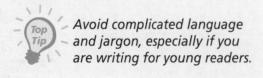 *Avoid complicated language and jargon, especially if you are writing for young readers.*

Persuasive language

Design a leaflet to advertise a new chocolate bar that does not melt in warm weather. You will gain one mark each for including a product name, a sentence about the benefits of the product, some factual information about price and availability, and a suitable picture.

 Top Tip *In a test you will not get any extra marks for drawing pictures on leaflets or posters if they have not been asked for.*

4

Understanding your reader

Here are some arguments you could use to promote a new brand of bike. Colour the three arguments red that would be more likely to appeal to people your age. Colour the three arguments blue that would appeal to adults.

1   The bikes are great value for money.

2   The bikes are the safest on the market.

3   The bikes come in a wide range of colours.

4   You can buy lots of cool accessories for the bikes.

5   The seats and handlebars are adjustable, so the bikes will last a long time.

6   Several celebrities own one.

6

TOTAL MARKS   10

Recounts

The language of recounts

Recounts tell the reader about something that has happened. A recount could be a piece of biography or autobiography about a historical event, or an account of a school trip or holiday.

Recounts are written in the past tense, with the events described in chronological order. They are often linked together with time connectives, which help to make the order of events clearer.

> **When** Mum was wrapping the presents we had to go upstairs. **Later**, we crept downstairs to see if we could work out what was inside them.

You might have to describe things quite carefully, but because recounts are non-fiction, they shouldn't contain imagery like simile, metaphor and personification.

Planning recounts

Recounts are quite easy to write, especially if you plan them carefully. Try using a time line or flow chart to list all of the main events in the correct order. It will save you time by making sure you write about them in the right order, without missing anything out.

Think carefully about which events to include in your recount. In a test you probably won't have time to describe every little thing that happened. Instead, pick the main events that influenced the outcome and leave out anything insignificant.

Key words | recount

The language of recounts

Add suitable time connectives to complete this recount.

We were watching TV when the lights suddenly went out.

_____ Mum checked the fuse box, _____ looking

outside to see if the neighbours' lights were out too. _____

she saw that nobody had any power, she found some candles.

_____ she found some torches. _____ the power

came back on.

5

Planning recounts

Read the time line and decide which events are important enough to be included in a recount and which are not. Cross out the three you would **not** include. You will get a mark for each of them.

7.30   Philip got up to get ready for his holiday.

7.50   He put on blue trousers.

7.55   He had toast for breakfast.

8.15   He could not find his passport.

8.25   He found his old watch while he was looking.

8.50   He found the passport.

9.55   He arrived at the airport, just in time.

3

TOTAL MARKS   8

Reports

Understanding reports

A **report** is a piece of factual writing about a particular subject. Information in reports is organised into topics, rather than chronologically.

Research your topic in books and on the Internet. Remember that there will be thousands of facts about your subject. It is your job to pick the ones that are most relevant to the report you are writing. For example, if you were writing a report about working children in the Victorian age, there would be no point including information about Victorian buildings, no matter how interesting you found it.

Once you have collected your ideas, use a spidergram or tree diagram to help you group similar ideas together in sections. Then work out how the different themes of each section connect to each other and put them in order. Then simply write a paragraph for each section of your plan.

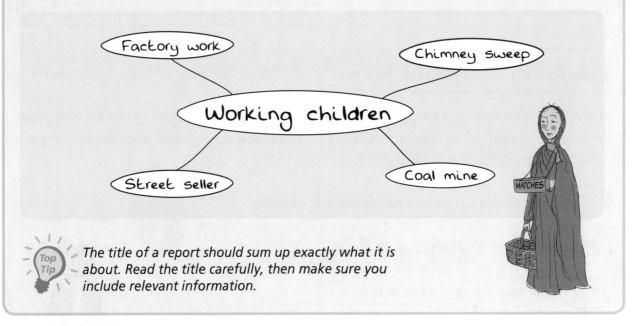

Top Tip *The title of a report should sum up exactly what it is about. Read the title carefully, then make sure you include relevant information.*

Report language

Reports are often written in the present tense, unless they are about a historical period.

They are non-fiction and fairly formal, so don't use imagery, slang or contractions. Think about whether you need to use any technical vocabulary that goes with the subject. For example, if you were writing a report about car engines, you might need to use terms like *distributor cap* and *head gasket*.

Key words report

Understanding reports

Look carefully at this spidergram. Some of the ideas are not relevant to the title of the report, which is in the middle. Cross out the four ideas that you would **not** include in a report.

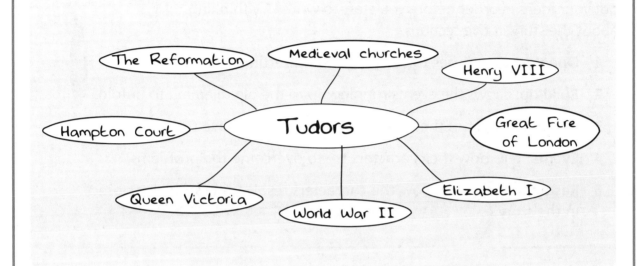

4

Report language

Imagine you are writing a short report to tell your classmates about a sport or hobby you enjoy. Write four sentences of your report, using appropriate language.

_____

_____

_____

_____

_____

_____

4

Planning stories

Planning a story

Planning a story will save you time in a test, by helping you to get your ideas in order before you start to write. Try thinking about the story in five sections.

1 **Opening:** introduces the characters and settings.

2 **Build-up:** allows the events running up to the big dilemma to unfold.

3 **Dilemma:** explains the problems the characters have to overcome.

4 **Events:** tells how the characters try to overcome the problems.

5 **Resolution:** explains how the characters resolve the problems posed in the story.

Openings

The best openings hook the reader straight away, with powerful descriptive words and lots of action. Try leaving a question unanswered in the first few sentences, so the reader has to keep reading to find out what happens next.

Top Tip *Try starting a story with one of your characters speaking, or a description of the setting or a character.*

Endings

Decide how your story ends before you start writing, so you can build up to the ending as you write. Try to leave your reader with something to think about after they have finished reading.

Here are some ideas for story endings.

- **Happy ending.**

- **Moral ending:** one of the characters learns a lesson.

- **Cliff-hanger:** characters are left in a dangerous situation with no obvious way out.

- **Twist in the tale:** something unexpected happens right at the end.

Planning a story

On with the show! A group of children plan a fundraising show to save a rundown local theatre, but things quickly get out of hand when the theatre's ghostly inhabitants join the cast.

Write a short plan for this story, in five sections.

Opening: _____

Build-up: _____

Dilemma: _____

Events: _____

Resolution: _____

5

Openings

Write the first four sentences of the story.

_____

_____

_____

_____

4

Endings

Write a sentence that explains what kind of ending you have chosen for the story and why you made that choice.

_____

_____

1

TOTAL MARKS 10

Characters and settings

Developing characters

Creating believable, realistic characters is the best way to hook your reader. Think about what each character would behave, sound and look like if they were real. If you spend time developing characters before you start writing, they will seem real right from the start.

Think about the role that each character will play in the plot and try to develop their personalities to fit. So if a character goes on a dangerous journey later in the story, make them seem brave and strong right from the start.

Top Tip

Remember, characters don't have to be people. Lots of stories have animals as characters.

Describing settings

The setting is the place where your story happens. Use imagery like simile, metaphor and personification to help your reader to imagine what your settings look, sound, smell and feel like. Match the setting to the feeling in the story at that moment and use imagery to create the right atmosphere.

You can have more than one setting in a story, especially if you need to change the feel of the story in the middle. Use connective phrases like *meanwhile, back in the mine,* or *later, at home* to move between settings, so your reader knows where the action is taking place. Try not to hop between locations too often, or your reader won't be able to keep up!

Developing characters

Imagine you are writing a story about two children who live in neighbouring houses. One is friendly, honest and reliable. The other is dishonest, spiteful and unfriendly. Write contrasting character profiles, for five marks each.

Character 1

Name: _____

Age: _____

Appearance: _____

_____

Behaviour: _____

_____

Special words and phrases to describe them:

_____

_____

Character 2

Name: _____

Age: _____

Appearance: _____

_____

Behaviour: _____

_____

Special words and phrases to describe them:

_____

_____

10

Describing settings

Now think about how the settings that the characters live in could emphasise their personalities. Jot down three creative words or phrases you could use to describe each character's house.

Character 1

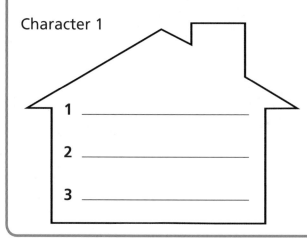

1 _____

2 _____

3 _____

Character 2

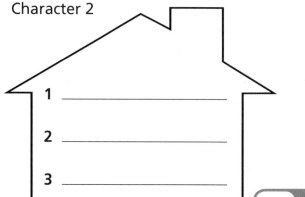

1 _____

2 _____

3 _____

6

TOTAL MARKS 16

Poetry

Writing kennings poems

A **kenning** is a way of describing something without saying what it is. You can make a kennings poem by joining together several kennings about the same thing. They are interesting because the reader has to piece together the different descriptions to work out what the poem is about. Verbs are usually very important in kennings poems, so make sure you pick good ones.

Age-counter,

Candle-lighter,

Card-sender,

Present-bringer,

Party-thrower.

Top Tip: *Try adding extra impact by turning your poem into a* calligram, *where the shape of the writing itself suits the subject of the poem.* **historical,** *funny!*

What do you think this kennings poem is about?

Writing haiku

A **haiku** is a type of Japanese poem.

Haiku always have 17 **syllables**, organised in the same way. Count the syllables in each line.

First line: 5 syllables.   Tiny ladybird,

Second line: 7 syllables.   Balances on blades of grass:

Third line: 5 syllables.   Then she flies away.

Haiku are very short, so they tend to be used to describe small but beautiful details, like a dewy spider's web or a pearly seashell.

Traditionally, they often contained a clue to the season they were about. The poet might mention snow for winter, blossom for spring, a mosquito for summer and falling leaves for autumn.

Top Tip: *Remember, a syllable is a beat in a word. Fly has one syllable, beetle has two, dragonfly has three.*

 Key words   kenning   calligram   haiku   syllable

Writing kennings poems

Write a five-line kennings poem about trees.

_____

_____

_____

_____

_____

5

Writing haiku

Read this haiku about spring, then complete the seasons by writing haiku for Summer, Autumn and Winter.

Spring

Blossom on branches,

Pink petals blown on the wind;

Summer is coming.

Summer

_____

_____

_____

Autumn

_____

_____

_____

Winter

_____

_____

_____

3

TOTAL MARKS 8

Glossary

abstract noun a noun that names a feeling or idea, e.g. happiness, sorrow

active verb a verb that describes who is doing the action, e.g. Eve ate the sweets.

adjective a word or phrase that describes a noun

adverb a word or phrase that describes a verb

alliteration a phrase where most or all of the words begin with the same sound

apostrophe a punctuation mark used for contraction, when two words are joined, or to show possession, e.g. We'll collect Dad's car.

author the person who writes a text

autobiography the story of someone's life that they write themselves

biography the story of someone's life written by someone else

blurb information on the back of a book designed to give the reader an idea of what it is about

calligram a poem written in a typeface which demonstrates the theme of the poem

clause a distinct part of a sentence including a verb

cliché a word or phrase that has been overused for so long that people have grown tired of it

collective noun a name for a group of things, e.g. a swarm of flies

colon a punctuation mark that can be used to introduce explanations or lists

comma a punctuation mark that shows when to pause, separates clauses, or separates items in a list

common noun a noun that names ordinary things, e.g. book, car

comparative adjective an adjective that allows you to compare two things, e.g. smaller, less exciting

complex sentence a sentence that contains a main clause and a subordinate clause

compound sentence a sentence that contains two equally weighted clauses, joined together with a conjunction

conjunction a word used to link sentences or clauses, or to connect words within a phrase, e.g. so, and, later

contraction when words are shortened, or two words are joined, by removing letters and replacing with an apostrophe, e.g. can't, won't

deduction the ability to use clues in the text to understand its hidden meanings

dialogue a spoken or written conversation between two people

direct speech words that are actually spoken, enclosed in speech marks

empathy the ability to understand the feelings and motivations of the characters in stories

fiction stories with imaginary characters, settings or events

first person events told in the first person are told from the viewpoint of the person doing an action, e.g. I am playing chess.

future tense describes things that will happen in the future

glossary a collection of useful words and their meanings

haiku a Japanese poem containing 17 syllables

imagery words used to build up a picture in a story, including simile, metaphor and personification

imperative a way of using verbs to give an order or instruction, e.g. Turn left at the traffic lights.

ISBN a unique number on the back of a book used by booksellers and libraries

kenning a way of describing a thing without naming it

main clause the main part of a sentence which makes sense on its own

metaphor where a writer describes something as if it were something else, e.g. The bird was an arrow, tearing across the sky.

narrator the person from whose viewpoint a story is told. May or may not be a character in the story

non-fiction writing that is not fictional, including information texts about real people and places, letters, instructions and reports

noun a word that names a thing or feeling

onomatopoeia when a word sounds like the noise it describes, e.g. crash, shatter

opinion what someone thinks or believes

parenthesis words added to a sentence in brackets to add extra information

passive verb a verb that describes the actions rather than the person acting, e.g. The room was tidied by Dan.

past tense describes things that have already happened

personification a writing technique in which human characteristics are used to describe non-human things, e.g. Shadows crept across the floor.

plural more than one of something, usually made by adding s or es, e.g. dogs, dresses

possessive apostrophe an apostrophe used to show that something belongs to someone, e.g. Sarah's homework

present tense describes things that are happening now

pronoun a word used instead of a noun to avoid having to use the same noun again, e.g. I, she, we, me

proper noun a noun that names a specific person, thing or place, e.g. Chris, Manchester, Friday

recount a report that describes events in chronological order, or the order in which they happened

report an information text about a particular subject

reported speech speech reported in a text, but not directly quoted, e.g. She said she was tired.

scan read quickly to find a specific piece of information

semi-colon a punctuation mark used to join clauses in a sentence where one adds information to the other

sentence a unit of text that makes sense on its own

simile where a writer compares one thing with another, using the words as or like, e.g. as bold as brass

simple sentence a sentence containing one clause

singular one of something, e.g. a bird

skim read quickly to understand the main meaning of a piece of text

speech marks punctuation marks that surround direct speech. Other punctuation goes inside them, e.g. "Goodbye," said Mum.

subject the person or thing in a sentence that carries out the action, e.g. Amy bit the apple.

subordinate clause a clause which adds extra information to the main clause, but does not make sense on its own

superlative adjective an adjective that describes the most of a particular quality that something can be, e.g. fastest, least expensive

syllable a beat within a word, e.g. di-no-saur

synonym a word with exactly or nearly the same meaning as another word, e.g. hot, warm

tense tells us when something is happening

thesaurus a book of synonyms

third person events told in the third person are told from the viewpoint of someone other than the person doing an action, e.g. She is working hard today.

verb a doing or being word, e.g. walk, sleep

viewpoint how a story is told from a specific character's way of looking at things

PAGE 7
Answering problems
1 £60
2 12.35kg
3 21
4 10

Multi-step problems
1 £264.10
2 Bag of 12 rolls: £2.24
   Offer: Buy 1 bag, get 1 bag half price
3 212g
4 £19.12

PAGE 9
Reasoning
1 6
2 78
3 276
4 70p
5 True. Add the largest 3-digit number.
   999 + 999 = 1998

Finding all possibilities
1 47 and 48
2 X = 1225 Y = 775
3 7 black beads
4 6.2cm and 8.4cm or 7.3cm and 7.3cm
5 $3 \times 7 \times 11$

PAGE 11
Number sequences
1 Rule: $+ 5$ Yes
2 Rule: $+ 3$ No
3 Rule: $- 6$ No
4 Rule: $- 4$ Yes
5 Rule: $+ 30$ No

Formulae and equations
1 $h = 8$
2 $y = 4$
3 $r = 7$
4 $4n - 2$
5 15

PAGE 13
Ordering decimals
1 9.841
2 1.489
3 8.941
4 1.849 or 1.894
5 1.489, 1.849 or 1.894, 8.941, 9.841

Negative numbers
1 12°
2 23°
3 11°
4 7 and −11
5 −11°C, −8°C, −4°C, 1.5°C, 6°C, 8.5°C

PAGE 15
Equivalent fractions
1 $\frac{3}{4}$ 4 $\frac{1}{3}$
2 $\frac{3}{5}$ 5 $\frac{2}{5}$
3 $\frac{3}{4}$

Comparing fractions
1 Any one of these fractions: $\frac{7}{8}, \frac{5}{8}, \frac{2}{3}, \frac{3}{5}, \frac{5}{7}$
2 Many possibilities. Check answer.
3 $\frac{4}{5}$ is larger because $\frac{2}{3} = \frac{10}{15}$ and $\frac{4}{5} = \frac{12}{15}$
4 Many possibilities. Check answer.
   E.g. $\frac{5}{16}$
5 Many possibilities. Check answer.
   E.g. $\frac{8}{15}, \frac{7}{15}, \frac{2}{5}$

PAGE 17
Percentages and fractions
1 70%
2 80%
3 76%
4 80%

Equivalent values
1 $\frac{1}{2} = 0.5 = 50\%$ 9 $25\% = 0.25$
2 $\frac{1}{4} = 0.25 = 25\%$ 10 $0.2 = 20\%$
3 $\frac{1}{20} = 0.05 = 5\%$ 11 $0.75 > 57\%$
4 $\frac{2}{5} = 0.4 = 40\%$ 12 $4\% < 0.4$
5 $\frac{17}{50} = 0.34 = 34\%$ 13 $8\% < 0.8$
6 $\frac{7}{10} = 0.7 = 70\%$ 14 $0.1 = 10\%$
7 $\frac{9}{100} = 0.09 = 9\%$ 15 $7\% = 0.07$
8 $\frac{11}{25} = 0.44 = 44\%$ 16 $\frac{2}{5} = 0.4$

PAGE 19
Ratio
1 6
2 15
3 16 litres
4 1 carton of cranberry juice
5 4:1

Direct proportion

1 butter → 150g, flour → 200g,
   grated carrots → 100g, sugar → 60g,
   beaten eggs → 50g, walnuts → 40g
2 225g
3 7.5cm
4 £7.50
5 0.06l or 60ml

PAGE 21
Factors

1 1, 2, 3, <u>6</u>
2 1, 3, 5, <u>15</u>
3 1, 2, 7, <u>14</u>
4 1, 2, 3, <u>6</u>
5 1, 2, 3, <u>6</u>

Multiples

1 2 and 4
2 3 and 9
3 2, 4 and 5
4 2, 3, 4 and 6
5 2, 3, 4, 6 and 9
6 2, 3, 4, 5, 6 and 9
7 36

Prime factors

1 $7 \times 3 \times 4$
2 $3 \times 4 \times 11$
3 $5 \times 11 \times 13$

PAGE 23
Rounding decimals

1
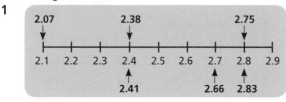

2 14
3 10
4 23
5 19
6 28

Approximate answers

1 9.3 and 6.5
2 7
3 16.5 litres
4 70p
5 False
6 11.78×5.19
   Rounds to 61.

PAGE 25
Adding decimals

1 approx: 591,   590.95
2 approx: 6.1,   6.072
3 approx: 67 or 67.5,   67.52
4 approx: 365,   365.14
5 approx: 11.4 or 11.45,   11.441
6 2.614 + 2.386, 2.792 + 2.208,
   3.281 + 1.719, 3.825 + 1.175
7 3.788 + 4.212, 5.179 + 2.821,
   4.183 + 3.817, 6.057 + 1.943

Subtracting decimals

1 4.36kg
2 0.958kg
3 3.45kg
4 C
5 B and E

PAGE 27
Column method of multiplication

1 7446
2 9016
3 9724
4 $253 \times 34 = 8602$
5 $415 \times 29 = 12035$
6 $517 \times 32 = 16544$

Grid method

1 5292
2 8808
3 10255
4 4750
5 189km
6 $284.2m^2$
7 £437.50
8 12775 litres
9 3.64l

PAGE 29
Written methods

1 55 lengths
2 41 tiles
3 4 pages
4 23 rows
5 42 boxes

Quotients as decimals

1 43.25cm
2 £468.40
3 22.75 litres
4 £6.75
5 258.6kg

PAGE 31
Fractions and division

1 48 chickens, 24 goats, 16 cows, 8 ducks
2 50p → $\frac{1}{2}$, 20p → $\frac{1}{5}$, 10p → $\frac{1}{10}$,
   25p → $\frac{1}{4}$, 75p → $\frac{3}{4}$
3 20p → $\frac{1}{10}$, £1 → $\frac{1}{2}$, 50p → $\frac{1}{4}$,
   £1.50 → $\frac{3}{4}$, 40p → $\frac{1}{5}$
4 £2.50 → $\frac{1}{4}$, £5 → $\frac{1}{2}$, £1 → $\frac{1}{10}$,
   £7.50 → $\frac{3}{4}$, £2 → $\frac{1}{5}$

Numerator greater than 1

1 $\frac{5}{8}$ of 32 < $\frac{3}{4}$ of 32
2 $\frac{2}{3}$ of 60 > $\frac{3}{5}$ of 60
3 $\frac{3}{4}$ of 48 < $\frac{5}{6}$ of 48
4 $\frac{6}{7}$ of 28 > $\frac{3}{4}$ of 28
5 $190 = \frac{5}{8}$ of 304
6 $342 = \frac{3}{4}$ of 456
7 $268 = \frac{2}{3}$ of 402
8 $291 = \frac{3}{5}$ of 485
9 $301 = \frac{7}{10}$ of 430

PAGE 33

Percentages of a quantity

1 £5, £15
2 £8, £32
3 £2.50, £7.50
4 £20, £2
5 £4, £2
6 £27, £54
7 £60, £720
8 £9, £27

Percentage decreases and increases

1 280
2 225 litres
3 672 chairs
4 £3420
5 540g
6 650ml
7 276 pages

PAGE 35

Using a calculator

1 51.8
2 18.2
3 79.5
4 511m^2
5 102.2m^2

Squares and square roots

1 1892.25cm^2
2 27cm
3 18
4 37
5 8.4

Using brackets

1 206.55
2 533.544
3 22.95
4 32.3
5 13.16

PAGE 37

Triangles

1 sometimes
2 never
3 sometimes
4 never
5 sometimes
6 always

Quadrilaterals

1

✔ ☐ ✔ ☐ ✔ ✔

2

	quadrilateral	not a quadrilateral
1 or more lines of symmetry	A C D	F G
no lines of symmetry	E H	B

PAGE 39

Parts of 3D shapes

1 2 triangular faces and 3 rectangular faces.
2 6 square faces.
3 4 triangular faces.
4 2 hexagonal faces and 6 rectangular faces.
5 1 square face and 4 triangular faces.
6 4 rectangular faces and 2 square faces.

Nets of solids

1 square-based pyramid
2 triangular prism
3 cuboid
4 tetrahedron
5 hexagonal prism
6 cube

PAGE 41

Moving shapes

1 rotated
2 reflected
3 translated
4 reflected
5 Check pattern.

Rotational symmetry

		Number of lines of symmetry				
		0	1	2	3	4
Order of rotational symmetry	1		D			
	2	B				
	3	E			C	
	4					A

PAGE 43

Positions on a grid

1 Check accuracy.
2 (3,–5) (5,–3) (5,1) (3,1)

Shapes and coodinates

1 (48,20)
2 (75,40)

PAGE 45

Measuring angles

1 79°
2 83°
3 160°
4 Check accuracy.
5 a = 35° b = 93°

Angles and shapes

1 x = 30°
2 p = 67°, q = 67°, r = 23°

Angles and lines

1 142°
2 85°
3 a = 65°, b = 115°, c = 65°
4 p = 131°, q = 49°, r = 131°
5 144°

PAGE 47
Units of measure
1 28 cupfuls   5 3.4kg
2 50 bags   6 29kg
3 30 days   7 1.4 litres
4 3 laps

Imperial measures
1 1.8m   3 10km
2 9 pints   4 4kg

PAGE 49
Area of rectangles
1 62.56m^2 2 151.2m^2

Area of right-angled triangles
1 Check area is 8 squares.
2 Check area is 15 squares.
3 Check area is 12 squares.

Composite shapes
1

2 217cm^2
3 142.76m^2

PAGE 51
The probability scale
1 $\frac{1}{2}$ or evens
2 Check answer – either certain or impossible, depending on the day today.
3 impossible or 0
4 $\frac{1}{2}$ or evens
5 certain

Equally likely outcomes
1 a $\frac{1}{6}$ d 0
   b $\frac{1}{2}$ e 1
   c $\frac{1}{3}$
2 A → 1 in 6 chance, B → 1 in 8 chance
3 Both have a 1 in 2 chance.

PAGE 53
Frequency charts and grouped data
Answers 1–3 are approximate.
1 43
2 97
3 26
4 Not enough information to say.
5 This is true.

Time/distance graphs
1 9.30
2 40km
3 10.00
4 0km (it did not move)
5 48km/h

PAGE 55
Mode
1 24   3 32kg
2 9.2cm   4 106

Median
1 34   3 322g
2 230   4 7m

Mean
1 34   4 520ml
2 0.6   5 8.4km
3 6.25cm

PAGE 57
Interpreting pie charts
1 interlocking   3 2
   plastic bricks   4 50%
2 $\frac{1}{6}$ 5 wooden bricks

Comparing pie charts
1 20%   4 False
2 $\frac{3}{8}$ 5 Ali
3 £10

PAGE 61

Planning for talking

Answers will vary.

Debating

Answers will vary, but one mark should be awarded for each point made.

Opinions

Answers will vary.

PAGE 63

The features of books

The covers of books include the name of the writer, or **author**, of the book as well as the name of the publisher. The back carries the **ISBN**, which is the book's unique identifying number.

Inside, the **contents page** lists the chapters or sections in the book, while the index lists the topics alphabetically to help readers find what they need. The **glossary** lists useful or difficult words and is found at the back of some books.

The choices publishers make

Possible answers include:

1   A publisher might choose to present some information as bullet points because they are clear and easy to read quickly.
2   Some information is presented in boxes to draw the reader's attention to it.
3   Publishers sometimes include a glossary to explain technical or unfamiliar words to readers.

PAGE 65

Reading fiction

Answers will vary.

Reading non-fiction

Children should tick each feature as they find it.

PAGE 67

Reading techniques

1   non-fiction
2   It is about the opening of a new cinema complex.
3   Seaward
4   Because Seaward is a holiday resort, so there will be lots of holidaymakers driving around the town during the summer months.

Using deduction

1   The writer is old. We can tell this because they use the phrase 'those of us who remember', implying that they have lived in the town for a long time.
2   The writer may not like the changes that have happened in the town, so they see the cinema as being to blame for them.

PAGE 69

Authors

Answers will vary.

Narrator and viewpoint

Answers will vary, but should be written from the point of view of one of the ugly sisters and take into account the knowledge that the sisters have within the story.

PAGE 71

Biography

Possible answers include:

1   Biographies are written in the third person because they are written by a writer about the experiences of someone else.
2   A biography does not give a complete account of someone's life, because the biographer can never know every detail of their life.

Autobiography

Possible answers include:

1   Using the first person makes the reader feel that the writer is speaking directly to them.
2   Answers will vary.

PAGE 73

Sentence types

Simple sentence: 1
Compound sentences: 3, 4
Complex sentences: 2, 5

Using sentence types

Possible answers include:

1   Simple sentences can help to draw the reader's attention to really important pieces of information.
2   Good: Compound and complex sentences can help to combine ideas.
    Bad: They can slow the reader down, because they have to work out how the ideas relate to each other.

PAGE 75

Writing contractions

Dear Katie,

<u>Hows</u> your new home? We're really missing you at school. <u>Your</u> lucky though because <u>wer'e</u> doing lots of tests this week. I <u>cant</u> believe it'll be Christmas soon. <u>You'l</u> have to come and stay over the holidays.

Take care,

Beth

Using contractions

Dear Sirs,

I am writing to complain about the service **we have** received in your Newtown branch. We purchased a kettle from the branch but when we got home we found that the lid **was not** in the box. The manager said **she would** replace it but we **have not** heard anything since then. I would be grateful if you could look into the matter for me.

Yours faithfully,

M Dawson

PAGE 77
Using possessive apostrophes

1   The men's cars were parked side by side.
2   The seals' enclosure was next to the penguins.
3   The women's suitcases were stacked on a trolley.
4   The two puppies' tails waved wildly.

Its and it's

Answers will vary.

PAGE 79
Commas

1   My aunt, who lives in Scotland, is coming to stay next week.
2   When the film had finished, we went out for pizza.
3   Anna, Rachel, Katie and Ruth sit on my table at school.
4   Yawning tiredly, Mark went to bed.

Colons and semi-colons

True: 2, 3
False: 1, 4

Parenthesis

Parenthesis has been used correctly in sentences 1 and 4.

PAGE 81
Direct and reported speech

Possible answers include:

1   Mel suggested that we should go shopping on Saturday.
2   "I was late because the bus broke down," explained Mark.
3   Direct speech allows your characters to speak to each other, which makes them seem more realistic.

4   Reported speech allows you to write about what characters have said, without them actually being present in the story at that moment.

Using dialogue to develop characters

1   "I want it now!" screamed the spoilt boy, rudely.
2   "Cheer up!" coaxed the little girl, cheerfully.

PAGE 83
Noun types

Possible answers include:

Common nouns: book, clock, house.
Proper nouns: Africa, Monday, Sarah.
Abstract nouns: joy, excitement, disappointment.

Pronouns

1   Kathryn and Liz are my friends although **they** live far away.
2   When my baby sister starts crying, I know **she** is tired.
3   Dad ran after the dog but he couldn't catch **it**.

PAGE 85
Spelling rules for plurals

1   foxes
2   trains
3   wolves
4   puppies
5   donkeys
6   tomatoes

Irregular plurals

1   species
2   men
3   antelope or antelopes
4   oxen
5   woodlice
6   teeth

PAGE 87
Using adjectives

Possible answers include:

1   A <u>tiny</u> bird sat on the <u>decaying</u> fence.
2   The <u>generous</u> girl gave her friend a <u>beautiful</u> present.
3   A <u>huge</u> storm blew <u>freezing</u> rain into our faces.
4   I was <u>exhausted</u> at the end of the race but <u>delighted</u> that I had won.

Comparative and superlative adjectives

	Comparative adjectives	Superlative adjectives
funny	**funnier**	funniest
flat	flatter	**flattest**
pretty	**prettier**	**prettiest**
expensive	**less expensive**	least expensive
exciting	more exciting	**most exciting**
generous	**more/less generous**	**most/least generous**

PAGE 89

Using verbs
Possible answers include:
1 said: announced, explained, replied
2 went: left, visited, travelled
3 ran: sprinted, jogged, raced

Verb tenses
1 Sam bought a newspaper.
2 Kate wrote a letter to her friend.
3 Chris and Daniel found a key on the pavement.

Active and passive verbs
Active sentences: 2, 3
Passive sentences: 1, 4

PAGE 91

Making adverbs work for you
Possible answers include:
1 "Who are you?" demanded the man, furiously.
2 Max gobbled the cake instantly.
3 Jane sauntered lazily in the sunshine.

Using adverbs
1 Bravely, the knight climbed the castle walls.
2 Carelessly, Gemma tore the paper off the present.
3 Furiously, Jake slammed the door.
4 Eventually, Tom found his football boots.

PAGE 93

Avoiding repetition
It was a hot day and we were soon hot and tired. We were all glad to reach the edge of the woodland and feel the cool woodland floor beneath our feet. As we began to pick a path through the trees, we began to hear the sounds of small creatures creeping through the undergrowth. As we got deeper into the forest, we started to feel afraid. We were afraid we would get lost, then Sam told us he had lost his compass!

Possible answers include:
1 warm
2 forest
3 started
4 scared
5 misplaced

Improving descriptions
1 Dad broke an egg into the cake mixture.
2 The rabbit hopped happily around its cage.
3 The hairdresser cut my hair.
4 The woman washed the little boy's dirty face.
5 Mum and I decorated the Christmas tree.

PAGE 95

Writing imagery
Possible answers include:
1 The wind struck the trees like a bulldozer.
2 The house was a lantern in the darkness.
3 The billowing laundry clung desperately to the line.

Avoiding clichés
1 The sun smiled down on the village.
   Possible alternatives include: The sun hung like a ball in the sky.
2 Our dog is as gentle as a lamb.
   Possible alternatives include: Our dog is like a playful child.
3 My science homework is a nightmare
   Possible alternatives include: My science homework refuses to be conquered.

PAGE 97

Using alliteration and onomatopoeia
Answers will vary. Possible answers are:
1 I bobbed about blissfully.
2 The crockery shattered as it hit the floor.

Reading alliteration and onomatopoeia
Possible answers include:
1 The writer has used the phrase *padded past, huge paws pounding* because it is alliteration and it draws attention to the size of the tiger's paws.
2 The word *growling* describes the sound the tiger makes and it is onomatopoeia.

PAGE 99

The language of instructions
1 Allow 7 working days for your order to be processed.
2 Keep your receipt as proof of purchase.
3 Cut round your design with a craft knife.

4   Use an <u>adjustable spanner</u> to tighten the <u>bolts</u>.

Organising instructions
Answers will vary.

PAGE 101
Persuasive language
Answers will vary, but one mark should be awarded to each of the following features: a product name, a sentence about the benefits of the product, some factual information about price and availability, and a picture.

Understanding your reader
Red arguments: 3, 4, 6.
Blue arguments: 1, 2, 5.

PAGE 103
The language of recounts
Possible answers include:
We were watching TV when the lights suddenly went out. **First** Mum checked the fuse box, **before** looking outside to see if the neighbours' lights were out too. **When** she saw that nobody had any power, she found some candles. **After that** she found some torches. **Eventually** the power came back on.

Planning recounts
The three events that are not important enough to be included in a recount are:
7.50 He put on blue trousers.
7.55 He had toast for breakfast.
8.25 He found his old watch while he was looking.

PAGE 105
Understanding reports
The ideas that would not be included in the report are: medieval churches, Great Fire of London, World War II, Queen Victoria.

Report language
Answers will vary.

PAGE 107
Planning a story
Answers will vary.

Openings
Answers will vary.

Endings
Answers will vary.

PAGE 109
Developing characters
Answers will vary.

Describing settings
Answers will vary.

PAGE 111
Writing kennings poems
Possible answers include:
Shade-giver,
Log-maker,
Leaf-bearer,
Nest-hider,
Branch-waver.

Writing haiku
Possible answers include:
Summer
Sun shines in blue sky.
Corn waving in golden rows
Ready for harvest.
Autumn
Dry leaves fall softly.
Red orange yellow flurry;
Rich gold tapestry.
Winter
Pale sun in grey sky.
Frost sparkles on bare branches;
Snow clouds gathering.

Letts Educational, an imprint of HarperCollins*Publishers*
77–85 Fulham Palace Road
London W6 8JB

Telephone: 0844 576 8126
Fax: 0844 576 8131
Email: education@harpercollins.co.uk
Website: www.lettsrevision.com

ISBN 9781844196975

Text © Paul Broadbent and Alison Head

Design and illustration © 2008 Letts Educational, an imprint of HarperCollins*Publishers*

This edition first published in 2012